MAKING THE RIGHT IMPRESSION

Making the Right Impression

Edited by

LYN RICHARDS

Home Service

Text copyright © Home Service 2007
Cover Design © James Haram

First published in the United Kingdom in 2007

Published by Home Service
48 Heaton Moor Road, Heaton Moor
Stockport SK4 4NX.

ISBN: 978 0 9555855 0 0

Book design and production for the publisher by
Bookprint Creative Services, <www.bookprint.co.uk>
Printed in Great Britain.

Contents

Introduction

In Deuteronomy 6 we read of a revolutionary plan, hatched in the mind of God, to ensure that Israel was an educated nation:

> These are the commands, decrees and laws the LORD your God directed me to teach you to observe in the land that you are crossing the Jordan to possess, so that you, your children and their children after them may fear the LORD your God as long as you live by keeping all his decrees and commands that I give you, and so that you may enjoy long life. . . . These commandments that I give you today are to be upon your hearts. Impress them on your children. Talk about them when you sit at home and when you walk along the road, when you lie down and when you get up. (Deuteronomy 6:1–2, 6–7)

Here we observe Moses as he describes the aims of Israelite education – God having his rightful place in the centre of personal and communal life, leading to obedience that in turn offers the promise of long and enjoyable lives for the people. Every education system makes promises to its graduates – in 1997 Tony Blair described education as his new government's best economic policy. For many in Western society, the promise of education is little more than economic prosperity. For Christians however the aim of education is to establish in ourselves and our children a focus on life which is God-centred. It is for this reason that Moses describes a system of education that begins with parents – these commandments are,' . . . to be upon *your* hearts' and only then focuses upon children. Parents themselves are then instructed to *impress* this God-centred worldview upon their children; the instruction is not merely to mention God once or twice during the week or even to ensure that they receive good Biblical teaching on Sunday. The writer of Deuteronomy is clear – the purpose of education is to firmly fix in children an awareness of the reality of a living God moving in history. In addition, the method and location of education is clearly described – as parents go about their daily business – when they get up in the morning, whether they go out and about or sit at home, when they go to bed at night, they are to breathe learning over their children.

During the last twenty years a quiet revolution has been taking place. Without formal approval from church leaders, without the support of large organisations or mainstream publishers and without the backing of wealthy benefactors, increasing numbers of Christians in Britain have been prompted to raise their children without sending them to school. Just how revolutionary this is, can be seen from the reactions of some church ministers, magazine editors and national Christian leaders who have looked at home-based learning with suspicion, dismay or outright opposition. And yet despite this lack of support, growing numbers of young families have chosen to use the home and the wider community rather than the local school as their primary places of learning.

This book contains their stories – or at least the stories of a very small number of those ordinary families who have chosen to do a quite extraordinary thing. As you read these accounts you will quickly notice that the typical home educating family simply does not exist. At a time when our state-funded schools are becoming increasingly monolithic in educational approach, with every child being expected to conform to a pattern set down by central government, education within the home education community is varied, vibrant and, genuinely, focused on how individual children learn. Time and again, within these accounts, the reader is challenged by the reality that children learning at home with their parents are more likely to have their educational needs met than those who sit in a class of twenty-five to thirty, vying for the attention of one adult.

One common feature that runs through this book is of families courageously choosing to be different. They have opted to swim against the educational and spiritual tide, often as a result, facing criticism from both secular educators and other Christians. Despite this, these accounts do not focus on negative experiences or criticism of those around them. Rather we read of families taking a step of faith similar in many respects to Abram's departure from Haran (Genesis 12:1). Thrillingly we also read of a faithful God upholding and blessing parents time and again as they attempt to walk a faithful path in raising their children.

Whether one is concerned with developing children's abilities or finding methods of learning that suit them individually, the home appears to be a powerful learning environment. Within these stories we read of children who are gifted and talented; not in the divisive, contemporary and narrow sense of possessing some special ability that sets them apart from their peers for particular attention, but in the sense that God gives *all* children gifts and talents that are to be nurtured and cultivated. Whilst schools focus primarily on academic performance, we see families exploring together to discover what each child is good at – whether these gifts are in the areas of music, sport, the arts, or practical abilities such as joinery or farming. Whilst school-based learning seems locked in a nineteenth century time warp with methods that would be familiar to Dickens' Mr Gradgrind, these parents write about exciting and innovative teaching methods that are sensitive to children's needs. In a very real sense these stories demonstrate the fact that parents working outside the system are the last true radicals in education within the UK.

After twenty or thirty years it is now possible to look at the 'graduates' of home-based learning and assess the success or otherwise of the venture. Of course, this does prompt difficult questions about how we can measure success in our young people. Can we honestly say, as successive British governments of either political complexion have suggested, that the sum of all educational success can be measured by the acquisition of five (or more) GCSEs at grade C or above? And can we hold that without this 'magic' collection of certificates our children are more likely to fall into a life of crime, disadvantage and poverty? It is certainly the case that home educated young people who sit GCSE exams often do exceptionally well. There is also a lot of anecdotal evidence that further education and sixth form colleges readily accept home education 'graduates' since they generally find them to be diligent, thoughtful, sociable students who appear to enjoy studying their chosen subjects. This, of course, knocks on the head one of the perennial arguments used against home education – that children taught at home are invariably going to be socially stunted and incapable of engaging with their peers. The fact is that both academically and socially, young people who have been educated outside school do well. American research maintains that they actually do better than their schooled peers![1] For many home educating parents however this is not enough. They aspire to more for their children. They want them to grow up with an understanding of the world and created reality that

---

[1] See *Home Schooling on the Threshold – a survey of research at the dawn of the new millennium* by Brian D Ray for detailed research findings regarding home-based learning.

firmly places God at the centre. Whether they are studying history or geography, science or literature, their desire is for each child to see the hand of God at work in his world. Like all Christian parents they aspire to see their children have a personal and intimate relationship with the Lord Jesus Christ; however, even if they have not yet made that commitment when they complete their home-based learning, home educating parents want to know that their children have a God-coloured perspective on the world. For many Christian home educating parents, this is the real measure of success.

For all the parents whose stories unfold in these pages, education is not a neutral activity devoid of spiritual intent. Non-Christian teachers delivering a secular National Curriculum are simply not consistent with a Biblical calling to impress upon our children a God-centred view of the world. For them, secular education is concerned with leaving God out in a vain attempt to be neutral. Such neutrality is nothing short of practical atheism; God, if he is there at all, is of such little consequence that he is omitted from all areas of the curriculum. In contrast, parents who share their experiences in these pages describe a view of the world and a lifestyle that is centred upon God; with such a view of reality it is little wonder that their view of education is fundamentally different from that which is the norm today. And yet, in these families, we do not see lives that are preoccupied with condemnation of what they see around them or even with protecting their children from a 'wicked' world, but rather we observe people who are focused on living out their Christian family life in a thrilling, dynamic way before an increasingly secular world.

The remainder of this book is something of a pot-pourri. More than anything else these twenty-one families present varied and vibrant approaches to education. All are Christians of a broadly evangelical perspective, but in other ways they are very different. Some are informal whilst others appear quite structured; some make extensive use of commercial curriculum packages whilst others use homespun curriculum individually tailored to their children's needs. There are stories of high academic achievement – GCSEs, A levels and further study at university whilst others tell of alternative routes with no formal qualifications at the age of sixteen. With such an eclectic mix of narratives it would be easy to slip into an almost judgemental mode, picking fault with those approaches that one most disapproves of. Remember, however, that these stories are little more than snapshots showing scenes taken from the complex lives of real people who are not afraid to live boldly. As a reader you are unlikely to agree with everything that you come across in these pages, however it is our prayer and our desire that you will be inspired to reflect on the experiences of these families and possibly consider afresh your own views on education and the raising of children.

Steve and Lyn Richards

Home Education,
An Exceptional Challenge

- Richard and Dawn Jones
- Children – two boys and one girl
- Age range between seven and fifteen
- Living in Cambridgeshire
- Have always home educated

We, Richard and Dawn Jones, have been learning at home with our children for the past fifteen years. Paul, our oldest, is at the time of writing fifteen years old; Ruth is thirteen and Barney is seven. It has been an incredibly fulfilling time, watching each child developing gifts and talents, and discovering what God has planned for them.

Why we decided to home educate

My mother set the seeds in me (Dawn) to home educate. When I was just a baby, she taught me not just how to talk, but was very keen to show me how the sounds related to the written word. This meant, as I was fascinated anyway, that I learnt to read at the same time as talking. I'm sure this wouldn't work for everyone, but it was great for me as I could read stories to my friends!

Interestingly, when I did go to school, I was so far in advance of my class that I did very little for the first year, in a large primary school in Nottingham. My teacher didn't believe me when I said I could read and when she gave me a maths workbook, I shot through it in a morning. She quite simply didn't know what to do with me.

How frustrating, when a parent has been able to achieve so much with a child, just to see it denied or suppressed. Unfortunately, I'm sure this isn't just my own experience. When my husband was at school he was told repeatedly that he would never learn anything, and so naturally enough, he didn't. This put in both of us a desire to bring out the best in our own children and we became aware fairly early in our marriage that home education was a valid choice.

One of our close friends had a little boy, Matthew, whom she had trained to be polite, opening doors for a visitor, etc. Within six months of his starting school, this had completely changed. His previously gentle, kind disposition had been replaced by violence and a disregard for his parents. Shortly afterwards his dad, a music teacher, was offered a job at a school in Canada. Both parents had been greatly concerned by Matthew's changed behaviour, and saw this as a chance to begin again. They taught both this lad and his sister at home for the first year and then joined a Christian school with about eight to ten pupils. When they came back over to visit, the reversal was dramatic. The gentle Matthew we knew was back, able to communicate well with adults and children alike.

Having seen this at first-hand, and also having learned a lot ourselves not just academically but through life, which we could tell and show to our children, we decided when Paul was very small that the best thing we could do was to teach him and any future brothers and sisters ourselves. The purpose of our lives has to be to love and serve our God, because of his wonderful grace towards us and we wanted our children first and foremost to have this priority straight.

How we started off

Although I always understood that a child is learning from his parents from the day he is born, I was rather nervous that I wouldn't do as good a job as was needed. I bought and borrowed numerous books on teaching – as cheaply as possible it has to be said, so charity shops were very useful! I was also concerned that Paul should be mixing with other children so when he was at nursery school age, I asked the parents of a small friend if she would like to come round for one morning every week to do some fun things with Paul.

It was all very formal to start with – everything was written down on a timetable that I beavered over for hours. We would start with a time of worship. Interestingly this is probably the item which has changed the least as we see it as a priority; it sets the tone for the day. I made a good investment at the Early Learning Centre in many small percussion instruments, and we used those some days; we made flags to use; dancing was encouraged.

For twenty-six weeks we spent time learning each letter.

- I recorded the BBC's *Words and Pictures* and used the appropriate recording for each letter – the children really enjoyed watching these,
- We used letters cut out of sandpaper for the children to be able to feel how the letters are made,
- I wrote lots of different letters on a blackboard for the children to spot the letter of the week in, and we always said the alphabet out loud and watched for the letter we were learning,
- I put sand or flour in a tray and let the children trace the shape of the letter,
- I drew a giant outline letter on our blackboard and let the children draw round it with different coloured chalks, to make rainbows.

We did similar activities for learning the numbers. For geography, I would sit with a book about somewhere abroad on my knee and we would 'fly' in our imaginations to this destination. In history, we read the story and then acted it out. They really preferred this to writing it all down, and I'm sure it has been remembered every bit as well. But for me the best bit of every day, and again, something we still do, is to read a book out loud. I had an old basket which I filled with different picture books, and let a different child choose a story each day. We started with simple ones, moving on to more mature stories and have now covered authors such as Enid Blyton, Laura Ingalls Wilder, Charlotte Brontë and C. S. Lewis.

All in all, Paul, and later on Ruth, really enjoyed doing these activities. Our blackboard was homegrown. I couldn't get a big enough one cheaply, so we bought some hardboard and some blackboard paint. Even now when Ruth tells her friends we sometimes use a blackboard, they say things like 'I wish we could, we have whiteboards and they're not as good!'

I did use a lot of pre-recorded schools programmes, so I could vet them first (witches were out and animals were in!). Radio programmes were used similarly, especially *Let's Move* (a BBC School Radio production), for physical education. Because of the way I work, I prefer to use a variety of methods, so we were never tied down to any one way of learning. We had all sorts of curriculum mixed up together; not specifically Christian, but if anything was opposed to what we believed it would be weeded out or reworked from our own viewpoint. We had little money to start with so most things came from charity shops or jumble sales. I can remember working out that we had spent £300 on bits and pieces through the year when I really started with Paul. Much of this was also for future usage and we didn't use everything!

Ruth joined in as soon as she was able, being two years younger. However this didn't hold her back and we found that she was learning at the same rate as Paul. It simplified things as I taught them both the same things at the same time, and still do. We keep roughly to the hours of 9.00 AM until 1.00 PM, with a break in the middle.

Part of home learning is to learn how to look after your home. We have always included housework in our plan. The most important goal in the morning is to get the washing out of the machine so it can dry and unload the dishwasher so that we're ready when dinnertime comes. The children each have their own jobs and earn money on a piece-rate basis.

It's important for us to include seasonal or current events in the plan. Christmas cakes and puddings are made together. Pancake day leads to some interesting results – this year we had blue pancakes when Paul used some artistic licence. Easter egg hunts were always a great chance for the children to practise their reading skills. We all learned about the development of a baby when Barney was born – a natural approach to, 'Where did Barney come from?' was far more preferable to the school teachings. Both Paul and Ruth made their own books about the new baby, with a picture of what the new baby would look like and what they thought he or she would do. Wonderful keepsakes.

Friday was always different – a trip out to places such as a nature reserve, the library or the swimming pool, would round-off the week. The children learned to look forward to the end of the week without realising that actually they were learning as much, but in another way.

How things have changed

Ten or so years on, and the family dynamic has altered subtly. Learning is less formal now, but then the older two can be given work to do and they get on with it themselves.

Barney (seven) has not been given much written work at all, just the Postal Bible School to be done each month. However he is bright and can read very well, and although I haven't sat down and taught him any maths, he figures out his own problems. He loves to play board games where money is used as he likes to be the banker! He can work out the change due without a problem. All sorts of games fascinate him, and he is learning extremely well this way, whereas sitting down with a workbook would be like a form of torture for him. Having said this, I will probably insist on some letter/word formation skills when the 'fresh start' comes in September.

Barney is probably the single most important factor on how well our learning day will go. He has the character type which says 'I will find out all I can about this world around me, no matter what the danger or cost'. If he is not kept active or engaged, he does the most annoying/danger-ous/challenging things! I have had my internet provider changed irreversibly, a phone call from the police to ask who had dialled 999, a call from the neighbour (friendly, merci-fully) to ask us not to squirt the hose over her conservatory, and many other misdeeds and challenging behaviours to deal with. However, supplied with the right books, interest-ing games, local children's clubs and a degree of freedom – well monitored – gradually we seem to be getting there.

Ruth is a good independent learner and it is very encour-aging that she can simply be given something to do and she will quickly work her way through. This means that she has more interesting things of her own choice that she can tackle when she has finished. In the afternoons she frequently visits the library to use the computers. She has figured out how to design a web page, and has set up her own web site. One of her God-given gifts is to dance and she has twice been involved in our church's guest service presentations. It is wonderful to see her determination in tackling whatever life may bring.

Paul – the non-academic of the three – is working one day a week with a friend of ours. Paul always has been better in work using his practical skills, so we jumped at the chance for him to train in plumbing. Having done a little research, he may well need a couple of GCSEs, as well as the experience, to get on to the apprenticeship scheme at our local college. For Paul this will be a real challenge! However hard he may find it, I believe it is important for children not just to do things that they enjoy all the time.

There is a need for discipline in life which can be encouraged by working systematically through something, and although it may not have been the most thrilling experience, knowledge has been built on firm foundations by the end. Paul finds it very hard to remember things. Through the past ten years, we have ingrained the four arithmetic rules, by diligently working on one example of each every day. This means that he will never forget them now. Patience is a virtue I always thought I owned in abundance until I had a family! But going over and over the basics again and again is what a child like Paul needed.

Paul has a great temperament, he is very relaxed in most situations and very good with small children. He has been extremely forgiving with his small brother, with whom he shares a room. All the minor events such as a display being broken or damaged, have been handled with pain but much grace on his part. I am convinced that it is this ability to get on with others that is tested to the full in a family, which will set him up for life.

More changes are coming to us because of the advent of internet trading. Selling on eBay has become a part-time job, soon to be a joint family enterprise, that we can tackle from home, with the hours worked completely under our control. This is a constant demonstration to the children of how to run a business, and they can have hands on experience at various stages of the process. The flexibility allows me to play a game with the youngest while I'm entering new auctions on eBay!

How we have benefited

Would I ever have done anything else other than home educate? No, but I have thought about it from time to time, just to make sure we were on the right track. Now is the most challenging time of all, being pre-GCSE, but exams are not all that is important in life by any means. It is more important to make sure that each child has good life-skills; that they can be independent when the time comes. Most important though is that they learn to love Jesus themselves.

To our delight all three children came to know Jesus at an early age. Interestingly, each was three years old when they made the decision, but all completely differently. Paul actually led Barney to Jesus when Barney was afraid of the dark one night. The older two are now regularly helping out with the church Sunday school and enjoy the youth work there too. They both have best friends who are Christians and they have purpose in their lives, with a long term vision of missionary work of some description in years to come. In the shorter term we are encouraging them to train towards a practical skill. Paul wants to go into a trade such as carpentry or plumbing and Ruth wants to train as a nurse. Both are confident and well balanced and though we have our moments, they are not just our children, but our good friends too.

We have had the freedom to pursue more outdoor activities than if the pressures of school were also bearing down. Paul and Ruth are strong swimmers, and Barney is very confident in water (except on his back, which we are working on!) The older two also enjoy kayaking with a local club and can do things I would never dare to attempt. Paul has just completed his Duke of Edinburgh bronze award with the

Scouts, and is now tackling his silver award. Ruth won a small talent contest with her dancing last year, and is looking forward to helping with the Powerpack children's work at two Christian camps this summer. Paul loves fishing, and Barney will no doubt follow his example. There has obviously been a fair outlay on these activities in time and money, but their confidence grows as they find they can achieve new goals and it gives opportunity to make new friends. It all happens little by little to start with, encouraging them in the small things will lead to greater successes.

There have been benefits for me personally as Mum, especially in terms of character development. Home educating is rather harder than going to a regular nine to five job because it requires that I change and adapt constantly and keep my temper in moments of stress. I have to be disciplined myself, if I am expecting my children to be; in fact that has always been an important principle behind what we have done – we can't expect them to have qualities in their lives that we are not showing in ours.

Our prayer is that each child will be able to do what God has planned for them and will not miss his best for their lives. When we were first engaged we prayed for the children that we would have, that each of them would come to know and love Jesus, and follow his ways. The fascination of seeing events unfold and God's hand on our lives has been and will continue to be a wonderful experience.

The First Step
Was the Hardest

- Steve and Lorraine Doye
- Children – three girls and two boys
- Aged between four and fourteen
- Living in North East London
- Have always home educated

When I married, I would have been amazed to think that we would become the parents of five children and besides that, to home educate them. I would have totally disbelieved that I could be happy and content with that sort of lifestyle. Our oldest child was a baby when we decided that our Christian friends weren't mad after all and that it was actually quite a good thing to home educate. There were two difficulties though, the task was daunting and so was the criticism. I wish that I could have looked to the future and laughed, both at myself and the criticism, but my knowledge and experience were too small. Instead we embarked on a fact finding mission.

Just how are you supposed to home educate? What do you do? What's a good resource when you see one? What about GCSEs? Is it so terrible to use a curriculum? My very kind sister, a teacher, took me to an educational bookshop. It was a blazing hot day, I had a toddler and a three-year-old in tow and there were lots of really good teaching books, but all of them were really only suitable in a classroom setting.

I felt overwhelmed, an imbecile and decidedly frazzled. We also visited experienced home educators. They didn't tell us how to 'do' a lesson either. I remained baffled but everyone in favour kept saying that I could do it; even people who knew me!

The turning point came when I met a missionary on furlough. She told me what not to bother with, lent me a resources catalogue and advised me to read Mary Pride's series, *The Big Book of Home Learning*. We thoroughly enjoyed volume one *Getting Started* and almost got to know the section on teaching styles off by heart. At long last we could begin to find some sort of direction. For purely selfish reasons, we planned to use the style called the Classical Approach. I thought that I would be best able to motivate and enthuse the children if I was interested myself, and this seemed the most interesting way to me. It was open to annual review, as was home educating itself.

Not living near any other home educators at that point, and still lacking confidence we decided to opt for a curriculum. Again, *The Big Book of Home Learning* was a great help. We tried the Covenant Home Curriculum on minimal information. Spending a lot of money on something unseen wasn't an easy decision. However, we loved it and so did Sophie.

I suppose that the crucial question is whether we have stuck with it. Ten years on we are still happily home educating and basing the schoolwork on the Classical Approach. This means that at the beginning stages we focus more on learning facts and mastering the basics. First of all, there is what is officially titled the Grammar Stage. It's rather like the little boy who can tell you every England player's batting average, ever. The next is the Logic stage and has more to do with learning to recognise why things happen as they do and also to detect falsehood. I suppose this would be the cricket fan's progression to knowing the individual player's strengths, the skills of the bowlers facing him and the inter-play of the two. The third is the Rhetoric Stage and the aim is to teach them to skilfully persuade others of their point of view. This would be like the family get-together when the subject of cricket is discussed. The contenders for who is the best player are debated and the youngster has to handle his knowledge and argue his favourite's claim in a reasoned and convincing way. There is an emphasis on studying classical works of literature, Latin and even Greek. We probably won't ever attempt Greek, but there is material available for parents who haven't studied Greek or Latin themselves. It's not as daunting as it sounds.

About six years ago we did have a diversion into the text-book approach because it was cheaper. A friend was using it successfully and enthusiastically, but it didn't work for us. We certainly learned a lot about perseverance in that year. It reinforced the view that we should stick with our own instincts as parents and not be swayed by how other fami-lies do things.

These days we can't afford to import curricula for four children, especially as many of the books are available cheaper (without teacher's notes) from Amazon.co.uk or discount US sites. The memories of excited children pulling schoolbooks out of boxes and studying a whole year's work in one afternoon while sitting on the hall floor are very, very precious. Moreover, as the years have passed, my confidence has grown. Some of the better workbooks are not available to us now, but that's something we have to live with and work around. We now base schoolwork on *The Well-Trained Mind* by Susan Wise Bauer. The recommended workload in our edition is ridiculously heavy, but with the benefit of experience, I realised this before I started. I have prioritised and left certain things out. Every year I worry about what we have missed, but schools don't cover everything either; just different things from us.

I have also found that the children aren't necessarily ready to do certain things when the general consensus agrees that they should. They were very resistant to learning to play an instrument, but this past academic year they have taken up both the piano and clarinet. They thoroughly enjoy music and are keen to practise. It is a major turnaround and I wonder why I had felt so much angst before. Another example of a situation where delay apparently caused no harm, was with beginning a modern language.

We have learned to be flexible and adapt. Well, I suppose that we have just had to get on with it! The children are different people and have different strengths of character and academic abilities. One of the children has a serious problem with concentration and so we have had to seek out old-fashioned books with factual explanations and minimal illustrations. To most people they're dull, however this child loves them. Fellowship has been invaluable in overcoming teaching problems. Others' experience and ideas have helped find a solution or put things into their proper perspective. Prayer support has never failed.

Educationally, the most important things that the older three children have developed are self-discipline, self-motivation and a love of learning. Children do change and become independent. They don't stay at the same stage for ever and each child matures at a different rate. It's much easier to struggle through a problem third, fourth or fifth time round when we know that we can see the fruit of the hard work, in the older children. It seemed overwhelming first time round though. It is incredibly rewarding to see children overcome a challenge or become absorbed in something that interests them.

When we chose not to send our children to school, we also chose to take full time responsibility for their social development. It can be wearing to be always on duty, always watching what they're up to. We are imperfect at it, but I'm convinced that it has prevented a number of disasters, has shown them that they really can avert a provocative situation and has made them face up to their own bad attitude before they act on it. On the other hand, it means that I have witnessed good things I didn't think they were capable of and enjoyed some very funny moments. Socially, the children are more confident than either of us were as children.

Spiritually, we are now entering the phase when they are able and willing to serve the Lord with their own gifts. It is what we had desired when we started out and is a source of great joy to us. So too is watching them choose wise friends who encourage them in the faith.

Perhaps we have learned more than the children. Academically, my knowledge base is far broader than it was ten years ago. God has done more than that and taught us about ourselves. Home educating doesn't allow any places to hide our weaknesses. In fact, at times it seems to highlight them. He has shown us that any achievement takes hard work, perseverance and faith, whether it's in character training or schoolwork. Our Heavenly Father has blessed us far more than we deserve and the rewards have far outweighed the cost. He has taught us how good and perfect he is.

Learning with LEGO

- Eric and Wendy Coates
- Children – two boys and two girls
- Age range from twelve to eighteen
- Living in Somerset
- Have always home educated

Whatever you do, work at it with all your heart, as working for the Lord, not for men. (Colossians 3:23)

Home education or home schooling, call it what you will, has become such a way of life for us that it is impossible to remember anything else! The seed was sown through our friendship with two American families living in England whom we met during our courtship and who were both, at the time, educating their young children at home. Soon after our marriage we moved to a new home and work so that when our first son Matthew was born in 1987 we rarely saw these good folks and we were certain that he would attend the local primary school in due course. However that all changed when Matt was about eighteen months old. In a conversation with a neighbour the subject of home education came up; I can't remember how. She told me that she had friends, both teachers as it turned out, who belonged to 'some organization or other' to do with home education and she'd make enquiries. Shortly afterwards she arrived on our doorstep with a bundle of past

copies of the *Education Otherwise* magazine. I opened the first
one and could not put it down – it was like a light had been
switched on and that here was a whole bunch of other people
doing what seemed so natural and right with their children,
without the need for school. So within a few weeks we joined
Education Otherwise (E.O.) and started to think more seriously and positively about this somewhat unusual, alternative approach.

Although it now sounds odd, and we were Christians
back then, I don't really remember spending hours in prayer
over the issue, or even thinking that we were choosing this
route for overtly 'Christian' reasons although we do strongly
believe that God guided and prompted and provided all the
right pointers during that time. I had always wanted to get
married and have a family (not an easy one for the careers
advisor at my old school) and when both those things happened I felt determined that our children should have a *real*
childhood, not one of starting school at four years old and
being 'tested' all the time, as was increasingly becoming the
norm back in the late 1980s and early 1990s. Eric, though a
little dubious, was very supportive and so as the magical age
of five started to loom for Matt we began to drop the idea of
home education into conversations with family and friends.
By talking to others our ideas took root and the more we
read, the more determined we became. Somewhat fortu-
itously we moved in the September of 1991, just as Matt
could have started school, so the pressure from folk who felt
we were mad and constantly asked, 'Haven't you looked
around the local school yet?' eased for a while. Once settled
into our new home we did visit the local school, but still
stuck to our decision despite the disapproval and concern of
a few.

By March 1992 when Matt turned five we were living and
working on a farm in rural Somerset and we had two other
children, Tom who was then almost three and Beth who was

just one. We returned from an Easter holiday with an agenda – Matt would start 'home schooling', Tom would get properly potty trained and Beth would learn to feed herself. I think the latter was achieved first! So I wrote out my little timetable complete with playtimes and, armed with a variety of books from completely non-specialist outlets, started the great adventure. Well, the timetable lasted a week at most, and the playtimes were definitely the most popular subject on it! This required a huge adjustment; of ideas and expectations, plans and pre-conceived notions of both education and what and how our child should be learning. And so over the weeks, months and the many years which have followed our approach has continually changed. As our children have grown, more changes were added to the home educational schedule and even now I often feel challenged to find new ways of doing things. One of the few consistencies from early days has been that most bookwork should be done in the mornings and by and large this has worked. Of course as the children get older more work may be required and more independent study is possible, so this sometimes happens in an afternoon, especially if someone has had a late start. I have one teenager who likes to stay in bed as long as possible! Another long-standing success, established I think once all four were being home educated, is a time after lunch when we all sit down and I read aloud. We've read so many lovely novels together this way, and certainly our youngest, Hannah, considers this the best part of home education. It has occasionally been a challenge finding a book to appeal to all – I remember the boys were more interested in *Anne of Green Gables* at the time of reading than the girls, but there are so many good books to choose from out there. . . . I've always found by bedtime I was too tired to read anything of any length anyway. At present we still home educate our sixteen, fifteen and twelve year old and have no plans to stop the read-aloud sessions. I can also remember a period when instead of a variety of subjects each day we tried a week of the 'maths on Monday, English on Tuesday, history on Wednesday' approach. This didn't last long either as we found so many things just overlapped, or a history idea would end up as a spelling lesson, and *nobody* wanted to do maths for any longer than they had to, so that idea quickly fell by the wayside. After all these years we do have a pattern to our days, but I still think the flexible approach has definitely worked best for us.

By keeping bookwork to mornings I hoped the afternoons would be free to do amazing craft projects, take long nature walks or do other stimulating educational things like visits to museums. The reality is, and has always been, somewhat different! We have certainly done our fair share of craft and, living in the country, we have enjoyed many a walk together. When the children were young it was not unusual for us to walk on our circuitous route once, or even twice a day. We have also occasionally been to a museum but on the whole, once we've read, the afternoon has become our time to do our own thing – housework, playing, reading or, many, many times, having friends over. It's a family joke that H.E. rather than standing for Home Education, actually stands for Home Entertaining, in our house!

If this makes it sound like every morning since 1992 has been a buzz of educational activity, let me hasten to assure you, and those who know us will concur, that this definitely is not the case. Whilst I like to have the ideal in mind and can get a little edgy when it regularly doesn't seem to be happening, we have had a great many days when all of it has gone 'out the window'. In fact we've gone for weeks when no formal education has taken place. For some this would probably spell failing, but we have come to realise that for us, this is not necessarily so. We soon realised that what children learn does not only occur between the hours of 9.00 AM and 12 noon on a Monday to Friday and that playing with a Lego set is only another term for design and technology. Learning comes in so many shapes and sizes and often just the little conversations in a day can be more instructive than three pages of an English workbook. I recall moving a *large* pile of cut logs from outside the garden to our woodpile with the help of the boys. We had an in-depth conversation about the holocaust and concentration camps, spurred on by our physical labour in warm conditions, which made us think of Corrie Ten Boom and the terrible conditions she experienced.

One thing our children have always been very good at, perhaps because they don't go to school, is asking questions. Whether it's a visiting plumber, electrician, or a neighbour cleaning his car, our children have always been there watching and asking questions. When we moved home and had someone to sand and repair a parquet floor the children helped and asked questions; when the tree surgeons arrived nine years ago to pollard some nearby lime trees, we had a day to watch and ask questions. It is no coincidence that the seed sown that day took root and our eldest son is now a qualified tree surgeon. Some of the most important influences in our lives and the lives of our children have been people they meet.

History has often taken place at our local castle on their special event days. From heraldry to Tudors to Victorians, we've enjoyed many living history events which have created an impact greater than any book, and our family holidays have always included visits to places of interest, working museums and so on. Of course we've had to face the danger of turning any day out into 'an educational experience' when we try to force the children to learn – getting the balance right also takes time and I've found myself having to just let them go and enjoy rather than stand and be taught! I truly feel, particularly when children are young, that no time is a waste, educationally. Children learn so much and through so many different media.

We have had no television for the last twenty years although we do now have one solely for use with videos and DVDs. This has been a good thing in many ways – the boys spent several weeks, along with Eric and me, watching the many parts of *The World at War*. It covered every aspect of World War II and was a much more acceptable way, to them, of studying history for a term! We learned a lot too. It has been good for programmes like *Pride and Prejudice* and *Emma*, when we read about the Georgians and Jane Austen. Living close to Bath helped too. As the children have got older and play has dwindled, a good video has been a nice way to unwind or to enjoy on a wet afternoon.

When we first decided to go ahead with home education we asked various teacher friends of ours about books they might recommend, particularly for maths. We also sent away for information about two curriculum packages. At the time we felt the expense of the packages was unnecessary, so we set about buying our own books, mostly from high street stores. We also found Usborne books to be a gold-mine of colourful fun and information and we re-used many of them over the years. One thing that has become abundantly clear over time is that all children do not learn in the same way, at the same pace or even with the same books. Like most home schoolers we have books on our bookcase that have never been touched, yet out of necessity have had to buy another reading scheme or maths scheme as child number two (or three or four) just couldn't make headway with the one already on the shelf. The common cry is, 'We need another bookcase!' We have two dyslexics in the family; one finding it much harder than the other and one child who finds most maths a complete mystery – but plods on regardless. This was not something for which I was prepared and at times I have found it hard to cope with and even harder to be patient with. However in each case I'm convinced the child managed better because they have been at home rather than at school, firstly because of the one-on-one help and attention and secondly because on the whole their self esteem has not been destroyed by their learning challenges or by negative comments from a peer group.

So, what happens when we get a bad day? If there is anyone out there who never has one, I'd like to hear from you! Whether it's caused by tiredness, PMT, frustration over a particular subject or just a stubborn child who won't write, we have our fair share of bad days. When they were younger I think our children always knew I'd lost it when I threw (yes, it's true) the tubs of crayons and felt pens across the floor and told them to sort them out. I could never understand why they couldn't keep the two things separate anyway. With hindsight I realised that I expected far too much of young children. After all it didn't bother them if the pens were muddled; only my adult mind was offended! Anyhow, on these days, sometimes after tears or temper, we usually give up and do something completely different. A walk always diffuses the situation, as does playing a board game together or just spending time apart – me in, them out, or vice versa. Bad days are all part and parcel of life and I guess I've always felt that at least the children see me, warts and all, just as I do them. Also being able to say sorry and have a cuddle is a really important lesson in life's journey. Our children know I'm not perfect but I'm still Mum and that has counted for a lot. As the children have grown, the bad days have become much less and I can't remember the last time I threw anything. However everyone is entitled to an off-day now and again – we just deal with it differently.

If we had a list of some of the most positive aspects of home education for us and how it has affected our lives, the time we have spent together would come right near the top. Although we never set out to be anti-school, but rather pro-family, when we see how little time even quite young children spend with their parents today, we are so grateful we were guided to this route and were able to take it up. By spending time together we feel we've really got to know our children (and them us) and this has been a great help, particularly as the teenage years have arrived. Another hugely positive aspect is the freedom to learn what we want, when we want and how we want and not being tied to the National Curriculum. So often we start on one topic and move on to another and another, all within a short space of time, following the children's questions and interests. If we were just supposed to be doing history or geography this apparent going off at a tangent may not have been possible. It has also been a great advantage to be able to go on holiday out of school holidays (cheaper and quieter!) and the lack of peer pressure to achieve a particular dress or behaviour code is also a great benefit. As those who know our children will confirm, they are very individual beings with their own unique sense of fashion, but are not easily swayed by the opinion of others. As one friend put it several years ago, 'he hasn't got the herd instinct', which we believe is something to be pleased about. It has also been a delight to see the children being children to a much older age than seems possible for those at school today. Lego sets, model play figures and dolls have all had much more long-term play value in our home than in many others we know and Hannah, who is twelve, still loves to dress up and play Victorians.

It would be untrue if I said that there is no negative side to home education. The responsibility of it can sometimes feel quite heavy, particularly if it is linked with pressure to achieve. We chose, as a family, and after much prayer, to go down the non-exam route for Matt. He is our tree surgeon son and our first 'experiment'. For him this was the better choice by far as although he would do whatever was asked of him in bookwork he was always happier outdoors making, building or fixing things or just generally being active. Once he was sixteen, we found him a one day a week

job to give him more experience and to expand his education. Staff at the local college were very supportive when we
enquired about courses and weren't fazed by his lack of
exams. Following an interview and some entry tests, he was
accepted on the course and thoroughly enjoyed it. With Tom
we felt perhaps exams would be more suitable so we purchased two correspondence courses, again after much
prayer. However once begun we fairly soon decided that he
wouldn't take the exams but just finish the courses, as we'd
paid for them! I now personally feel for us and our family
that the pressure to get these courses done has been a negative influence on our home education and Tom's love of
geography (he used to sleep with an atlas under his pillow)
has definitely been eroded by having to do written assignments. At the present time I can't ever see us going down
this route again, although I appreciate this is very personal
to us – we certainly know plenty of home schooled young
people who do exams and do very well at them. They are just
not for us. That said, Tom now attends the local college one
day a week, studying for a computer systems support
diploma. After his interview and entry tests they told us they
would take him on the course as he was already mature
enough (having previously been told they really didn't take
sixteen-year-olds straight from school as they were too silly).
I think this boiled down to the fact he could communicate
with an adult – something that must rank as one of the most
commented on facts about home educated children. Tom
continues to learn at home, but then . . . we'll wait and see.
Whatever happens we know God will provide and honour
the choices made.

On a less serious note, I always felt a bit sad that I would-
n't get school photos (really) and was concerned about team
games. The former I've coped admirably without and the
team games have been resolved in other ways. The local
primary school only had twenty-six pupils anyway so team

games there would have been a bit limited! Both boys loved football and having been coached by Eric in the back garden since they could kick a ball, joined the local town's youth football team for their age group. They have spent several years playing, but this year both have resigned to make way for other things. The girls have attended a local gym class (no exams!) since age five and love it. They also had a spell of trampolining. Their one foray into team sports – netball – ended in disillusionment, with the attitude and snide comments of the other young girls there, so they left. All four have learned to swim and play badminton, of a kind, in the garden.

I feel very much that the friendships our children have made over time have been *real* friendships, not just the result of being thrown together in a classroom with thirty others. Disagreements are rare and there is a general air of wanting to spend time together and do things with their friends. They mix happily with boys and girls alike and have friends of various ages – our youngest daughter at twelve writes regularly to two or three much older teenage girls and one of their good friends is eighteen. We have been blessed with many friends as a family and over the years our circle of home educating Christian friends has grown, whether living close by or much further afield. They have offered invaluable support and friendship; without them life would be much poorer.

Finally, although I have written this from my perspective, none of it would have been possible without the love, support and commitment of Eric who, after his initial wonderings, is now totally convinced of its rightness. He has always been there, never criticized, has given the children lots of hands-on learning opportunities on the farm, helped with bookwork when around and has stood up and defended us against sceptics and critics. Last but not least, he is an amazing chauffeur to us all!

I recently asked our boys individually, now they are eighteen and sixteen, their memories of early home schooling. Without hesitation they both replied 'we played outside when it was nice, and built models with Lego sets when it was wet!' As both are relatively numerate and literate we must have done something else too; but I feel that, if this is the main thing they remember, then our aim to give the children a *real* childhood has been achieved. God has guided and provided so much along the way – we are so grateful for his direction into home education and wouldn't change it for the world.

Like Trees Planted by Rivers of Water

- Clive and Ruth Davies
- Children – two girls and one boy
- Age range between seventeen and twenty-two
- Living in South Shropshire
- Have always home educated

Then Moses said to Him, 'If your Presence does not go with us, do not send us up from here'. (Exodus 33:15)

God leads different people in different ways. We had our first gorgeous about-one-year old, all blond and podgy and full of smiles and increasingly full of chatter. As we are always trying more and more to submit all of our lives to Christ's rule, we asked ourselves what the Lord wanted us to do about the education of this as yet small bundle of – for the most part – joy. When Clive got in from work and Eleanor was in bed, we brainstormed and wrote down what sort of education we thought was best in line with the Bible's teaching about the nature of man, the world, the family and God. Then we considered which of the schools and nurseries to which, geographically or financially we had access, provided an education most closely aligned to our ideal. None was very close!

What did we look for? We looked for a wide-ranging education reflecting the richness and diversity of God's world.

41

We believed that, being firmly rooted in a Christian philosophy, this wide curriculum would also be well integrated. We
looked through the Bible and particularly in the Pentateuch to
see how God taught his people. We saw there discipline, motivation and reward. We saw observation, repetition, recall and
understanding as being core steps to aim for. We saw creativity and experimentation. We saw the great Teacher directing
the process and using lots of hands-on activities. We saw our
role as helping to form, under God, a set of values and attitudes, building good habits and developing skills. This would
mean that the children, if converted, would be useful to God's
work and be as flexible servants as possible. So, for example,
a broad education, perhaps comprising the 3 Rs as well as art,
music, astronomy, literature, citizenship, sport, and providing for interactions outside the Christian family, meant that
the child would have more awareness later on and a greater
experience to draw upon when choosing where to specialise
or what career to pursue. But where to find this ideal education? That was the question. . . .

One nap-time I, Mum, was ironing and listening to
Woman's Hour on the radio. I heard about a lady in Ireland
who had educated all of her eleven children at home for at
least part of the time. I followed this up eagerly, obtained her
book, which I read as a thirsty man in a desert drinks on
finding a spring! Was there a possibility here? I followed up
the contacts provided at the back of the book, to Education
Otherwise. Thence I made contact with Susan Schaeffer
Macaulay and read her book, *For the Children's Sake*; I was
fast becoming sold on the idea of home education, not for its
own sake but because it gave us the freedom to try to do
what we believed God wanted us to do with the children we
had. Clive had to go to Bristol on a business trip and suggested baby Eleanor and I go too so we could have some
days away together with travel and accommodation paid
for! On a free afternoon we walked in pouring rain around a

nature reserve, with Eleanor in a backpack. We dissected the whole idea and discussed with tremendous intensity the pros and the cons, and it was there that we decided to go for it. Not that we told many people of course! We were extremely wary of their reactions and certainly didn't want to seem to criticise our parents who had put a lot of thought and care into our own education.

The next excitement for us was thinking the whole task through, finding books which advised about what children should know by what age and stage, defining our goals in more detail and researching materials. These were pre-computer days for us and research was slow as I phoned the USA and awaited impatiently the arrival of sample materials. We knew no one else who was interested in following this weird course, until a visit to a Christian college friend and her family brought the news that they had taken their son out of nursery and were thinking about 'doing it themselves'. Was I excited? Since then we have shared ideas, plans, books and children with much thankfulness. So at least there were two families this side of the Atlantic doing home-ed!

We chose Alpha Omega materials as they provided work books for science, social studies, English and Bible. We used Heinemann Maths and, feeling as if I was steering an ocean liner in the dark, I tentatively set off. Mercifully there was an invisible but very experienced Pilot standing with us and we were kept from some of the worst shipwrecks. The work-books were useful as an introductory style of teaching and learning, but my confidence soon grew and we wanted to vary the approach. We realised that although that approach *might* be the best for this particular child, not all children learn the same way and we wanted to have a variety of methods on the go. We bought Bob Jones University Press material for science and music and used material from A Beka Book for spelling and health, safety and manners. It was a temptation at that stage to keep switching to new

courses as we discovered them, but we decided that changing would be disruptive on the – by now two plus – children
and would interfere with the coverage of material, so we
only changed once or twice during their primary years. We
think that this decision was the right one, having done very
careful research initially.

We, but mainly I, learned some important lessons through
the frustration of constantly changing from what I thought
good to what I thought best: consistency, perseverance and
progress, which are all blessings. It's good for a child to see
their progress as they move from book one through book
two to book three of a good scheme in any subject. It's good
to train up persevering, not butterfly-like, students. A great
deal of money can be wasted on changing schemes each
year, even though it may be done with the best possible
motives. We think it is important to find a good scheme for
each subject, preferably not the same for all subjects and
stick with it, even if something 'better' comes along and
catches the eye. Another hard lesson for me was that I could-
n't teach the children everything and that there would be
gaps. My aim had to be to foster the curiosity and skills that
would enable them to find and fill their own gaps.

You may wonder what reactions we got as we told people,
particularly the family and the church what we were going
to do! Throughout the home education of our three young-
sters we only verbalised our intention to home educate a
term at a time. This gave us more 'space' and diluted the
horror that relatives and onlookers felt at our nonconfor-
mity. It was always, 'We'll see how it goes this term. You
never know . . .'. For of course, as Christians, we know we
never do; but God does. My sister's response was the one I
recall the most vividly. We were walking buggy by buggy
back towards our house when I dropped the bomb. She
stood stock still, looked me up and down, as if to reassure
herself she was walking beside the person she had thought

and finally said, 'You're NOT!?' The strength of her excla-
mation blew me several steps backwards, but when I had
recovered and assured her it was, 'just for a term to see how
we get on', she was slightly mollified! My parents 'reserved
their judgement', and have been very supportive, whilst
being careful to support my sister in the schooling of her four
too. Clive's parents were interested and supportive of our
plans and I remember my father-in-law hearing the children
saying their tables and pronouncing, 'There can't be much
wrong if they can say their tables like that!' I'm not saying I
agree with him, but it was a relief to have him say it all the
same! We've tried to be sensitive with professional teachers
in churches we have attended and with families who felt
they couldn't home educate. We believe that kindness,
humility and justice are bigger issues than home education,
when all's said and done.

We have experienced so many mercies and providential
provisions on our home schooling journey that a book
wouldn't hold them all, but to give a few examples: just as
we began to think about what the children were missing
through not being at school and could only think of team
sports and group musical activities like orchestras and
choirs, we discovered that the local sports centre ran a
netball club which Eleanor could attend and so learn to play
as a team member. Later Bernard was able to play rugby and
football similarly, although he had Sunday match issues
which Eleanor never had. We discovered a monthly music
club for junior primary folk which provided a fascinating
introduction to a wide range of instruments and enabled
Eleanor (and probably the others later, I don't remember) to
play 'Twinkle, Twinkle Little Star' in a Christmas concert on
her recorder! Later on they were able to join the county
orchestra. As they grew older I found out about opportunities for them to participate in Brownies, Guides, Cubs,
Scouts, the Duke of Edinburgh's Award scheme and Cadets.

However, these activities are only as good as their leaders; like fire, they make good servants, but bad masters! God has been totally faithful. He gave us the vision and has provided in every way, at every step of the way.

What about secondary level education? Here again we were very blessed. Our children went straight from their steady and fairly consistent primary education to start studying for GCSEs, which we then took over a number of years. We took a less important one, IT, first, feeling that it didn't matter much if it went wrong. We were able to take this, Eleanor and I, at a local sixth form college evening class, and thus began our computer literacy. I shall never forget the fun of those evenings and my eleven year old daughter beaming over at me on the computer next door to hers, 'Are you stuck *again*, Mummy?' she would say, and then she'd proudly come over and un-stick me! But she got her GCSE and then the next year took two or three for which I think I taught her and so went on to gain ten or eleven good GCSEs. She finished these early and was able to take two A levels at home before going on to a sixth form college. She had decided that the only degree she really wanted to study was medicine. So I found a book published by Mander Portman Woodward entitled *Getting into Medical School*, which I perused until I had sucked it dry! But it did the trick and nudged us in the right direction. She went to a sixth form college where she did very well. In fact she got a scholarship on the basis of her GCSE grades and dates and an interview. Eleanor is now happily in her fifth year at Cambridge, loving medicine.

Bernard was quite a different character, very physical and a creature of the outdoors! He studied at home to sixth form level too, but with him it was a battle from his earliest days. First it was writing, then spelling, next how much he would write. He had moments of enthusiasm, but Eleanor had been an easy start and I began to see that not all children were like her! Not by a long way! Bernard and I are very like each other too and this has meant that a lot of the battles have been personality induced; but whatever their cause, a lot have ended in tears or in my having to phone Clive to get him to have a word with his son. No, that hasn't been easy, but Bernard himself states categorically he wouldn't have done as well if he'd been at school. He's reading Agriculture at Harper Adams College in Shropshire and enjoying that as much as he ever enjoys academic study, which isn't much! But he does love the animals and he's got a good practical brain on him.

Our baby, Hilary, is different again – probably the brightest of the three but without strong academic ambitions and looking forward to getting married and having children of her own. At sixteen we feel it is probably a little early for that! She too did GCSEs at home and two A levels before going on to sixth form college where she is studying with a view to reading English at university. Universities don't mind home educated students. We wondered about O levels versus GCSEs versus no qualifications, versus just going straight onto A levels. But finally, deciding that our three were likely university material, we felt that GCSEs would stand them in the best stead. Doing subjects like English and English literature at home meant that we could largely choose the texts studied. We didn't feel that GCSEs were in themselves a bad option nor that they were of a very high standard academically, although they could be supplemented!

This has been by way of an overview! I could have majored on how we set about doing GCSEs, or why we did them *when* we did, or how hard A levels are, or why we encouraged the children to go as far as they could academically, or how we dealt with their 'socialisation' but I want to finish up where I started, the purpose of home education: to what extent have we achieved our goals? Well, by God's grace the two girls are both saved and enthusiastically looking towards how they can serve the Lord wherever they find themselves – in a university Christian Union, in a church crèche, leading a girls' Bible study on purity and relationships, in bringing international students into contact with the gospel. At the same time we really are best of friends. It's been wonderful seeing Hilary maturing as she lives away from home in a Christian family whilst at sixth form in Cambridge and knowing that Eleanor's there for her to invite her to tea, take her to interviews, advise her about Christian behaviour or explain something in the Bible to her.

It's wonderful seeing all three appreciate, as they grow older, what home educating them has meant to us and to see their growing appreciation. Bernard also has a good relationship with us and it's good to see him coming to his dad for advice on his finances or with his car. He does not make any profession of faith at present, but we trust that God may yet bring him in so that we are *all* family twice over!

We could recommend books, suppliers, support groups, methods, habits, regimes and timetables, but our strongest recommendation is to seek God in his word, and daily to pray as Moses did for the presence of the Lord, minute by challenging minute.

A Choice Worth Making

- Mark and Jenny B
- Children – four boys and one girl
- Age range between five and seventeen
- Living in Cheshire
- Have home educated for nine years

It was a sunny autumn morning as Mark and I strolled through the village he grew up in. We were planning our forthcoming marriage that December and musing over the children we hoped to have. The conversation drifted to what school would be like for them. What if the Lord called us to service overseas? Where would our children be educated then? From out of the blue Mark suddenly stated, 'I think our children should stay with us whatever we do and learn through real life – that would be far better than any school'. Somewhat horrified I replied, 'No, no, no, children need school – it gives them routine! They need school uniform.' I thought that his was a crazy idea and secretly sent up a prayer that the Lord would not call us overseas!

Our first child was born two years later and we realized that what we wanted most for this child and any subsequent children was that they should come to know Jesus as their Lord and Saviour for themselves. We wanted their Bible knowledge to far exceed our own and for them to grow in an atmosphere of love where Christian values prevailed.

As Richard, our son, grew it wasn't long before we began looking round for a local playgroup – we had ruled out nursery as too all encompassing. Richard settled in well, but gradually, as the weeks went by, we began to realize that we didn't like some of the attitudes that prevailed at the group. A blind eye was turned to some bullying in the name of 'boys being boys'. Parents were only welcomed at times that suited the playgroup and the leaders would tell you confidently about your child as if they knew him better than you. When we realized that many of these attitudes would be carried on to the local primary school we began to pray and search for alternatives.

We knew of a couple of Christian schools and so began looking at the concept of Christian education. At the recommendation of someone connected with one of these schools we bought and read the book *Curriculum Unmasked* by Mark Roques. This revolutionized our thinking and made us realize that we wanted a Christian education for our children with Christ at the centre of everything.

On the basis of this decision we moved house to be near a small Christian school where our first two children were involved for a few years. Although there were many positive aspects of this school, we began to realize that even in a small school individual needs cannot always be catered for. As our eldest son entered juniors he began encountering problems and suffering from stress caused by the working practices of the school. Once more we began considering our options and this time viewed two local primary schools. We even filled in an application form for one of them. However, we realized that we could not fulfil the biblical mandate given in Deuteronomy 6:7 by sending them to a secular school.

It was at this point that we read an article in a woman's magazine about a lady who had taken her children out of school in order to teach them at home. She was just an ordinary woman with no qualifications except that of loving her children. Could we do this? I was expecting our fourth child and Mark's job was increasingly more demanding. We prayed. The Bible has a simple answer to worry. 'Seek first the kingdom of God and His righteousness and all these things will be given to you as well'. We knew that we had to seek God's kingdom first and foremost for our children and that for us it meant teaching them at home. Having made this decision our hearts felt at peace and we trusted God to work out the practicalities.

We joined the home education support groups Education Otherwise and the Home Service, then armed with their contact lists, began getting in touch with other local home educators. As we met with more of these folk we began to realize that there were as many ways to approach the task ahead as there were families. We started to wonder which approach would best suit our family and once again we found ourselves searching for answers. Home education should come with a health warning as follows: 'Warning: Home Education can make you seriously think!'

In many ways we had an easy start to home educating. We had two boys who worked and played well together and who could already read. We had a pre-schooler who played well alone and still took afternoon naps and understanding friends and family nearby. After six months we felt confident we'd made the right decision. Our eldest son blossomed again and we were able to cope with the extra workload.

However, the birth of our fourth son rocked the boat a little. He exploded into the world at 11lb 4oz wanting lots of attention. Our placid three year old decided to drop his naps and get in on some attention seeking and the home education novelty had worn off a little for our two oldest. Our routine was definitely shaky now. Was this really the best thing for our children? We decided to stick out the year and attend a weekend conference for Christian home educators run by the Home Service. We reasoned that we might find some coping strategies here and keep going or else we would find a bunch of maladjusted weirdos in which case we could try the school option again.

We were totally unprepared for what we found at the conference. Here were a group of people the like of which we had never met. What a blessing and an encouragement we had. These parents were neither hankering after designer apparel for their children nor striving after high-powered jobs. They simply loved their children and were concerned for their *total* well-being – physical, mental, moral and spiritual. They put the Lord Jesus at the centre of their families and loved sacrificially. The results, as shown in the characters of the children, were amazing. Here was a group of children who were polite, fun-loving, respectful, courteous and disciplined who could hold conversations with both children and adults alike and who actively wanted to be helpful. Many of these children had already made decisions to follow the Lord Jesus for themselves and it showed. An abiding memory is of never having to struggle through a door with the pram – it was always opened for me by older children without me ever having to ask for help.

We left that conference feeling not just a part of a network of home educators but part of a family of like-minded Christians who stretched the length and the breadth of the UK. Over the ensuing years we have made firm friendships with many of the families we met at that first conference and our children have benefited enormously from having friends who share the same faith and a similar lifestyle.

So what is home education like in practice for us? I have certainly discovered that my children do not need school uniform and what a relief that is when you're behind on the washing!

What about routine? Well, we have found routine to be useful although it is our slave and by no means our master. Who can resist building jolly snowmen on the only white day in winter whilst droves of school children are confined indoors, or accepting an invitation to a friend's farm so the children can climb trees and *really* learn about creation. Routines have also changed with the seasons in life such as a tiring pregnancy, a boisterous toddler, a family bereavement or a sixteen year old turning the kitchen into a science lab for his GCSE coursework.

Home education is a total lifestyle choice. It is not something you can put into a nine-to-five box or separate from the rest of daily life. It is a sacrificial life in many ways. For most of us it means living on a single income with times of loneliness. Attending a Mums and Tots group with a mass of school-age children now becomes impracticable and the term 'popping to the shops' with an ever increasing brood in your sole care is just a joke. There are times of frustration when a child just can't grasp a new concept and times of feeling totally overwhelmed by the sheer enormity of the task which has just got worse by the washing machine breaking down and a crabby baby throwing up over the last of your clean jumpers! Why would anyone continue with such a demanding lifestyle?

However, despite these difficulties on a daily, weekly and monthly basis we can testify to God's unfailing goodness to our family, as we have tried to 'Seek first His kingdom'. God has indeed added many good things to our own lives and those of our children. Good gifts come in many different shapes and sizes and we have experienced a practical meeting of our daily needs; an encouraging phone call at the right time, an answer to prayer for material suitable to help teach a struggling child, a shoulder to cry on, as well as material gifts. More important than this our faith and characters have been developed as we have learned to 'trust in the Lord with all your hearts' and to 'lean not on your own understanding' and to believe that God alone can make our 'paths straight'.

A major incentive for us to keep going has come from seeing our family develop very close relationships with one another in a way not always observed in non-home educating families. Younger siblings, despite being irritating at times, are loved and cherished and indulged a little. Older siblings are people to look up to and aspire to. Family holidays are special times of togetherness instead of juggling acts trying to resolve the interest of toddlers and teenagers. The family meal table is a rich time of sharing. It has also been a joy to have each child snuggle up to me and ask what Jesus has really done for them and then to have the privilege of bringing them to the Lord.

We set out with a desire to seek something better for our children but there has also been a knock-on effect on our church and community. Our children have been asked to participate in events at church because of their positive input and maturity and it gives us great pleasure to see our children integrate fully into church life rather than only feeling comfortable in a youth group full of their peers. People who know us have stopped asking us, 'What about socialisation?' The uninformed still get the answer, 'Yes, it's a real problem for school children, they never seem to learn how to relate effectively to adults or anyone else a year either side of their own age!' Despite some scepticism from others, and with some help from outside tutors, our eldest son managed to achieve an excellent set of GCSE results and we felt that he was mature enough emotionally, academically and spiritually to cope with going to the local sixth form college. Mark has become a college governor and our eldest son has continued to do French at home which helps to keep us involved in his education. At a recent parents' evening we were somewhat surprised and delighted by one of his tutors who enthused about our son's character and finished with, 'Of course I can tell he went to the *very best* school!' Who were we to deny such a statement?

Sure, we work hard in the daily business of raising our family but ultimately any success or glory must go wholly to our loving Heavenly Father who has given us blueprints of parenthood and daily living in the Bible.

Home education has made us think 'outside the box'. Many areas of life which we so often take for granted have come under the microscope and have been reviewed from a biblical perspective. We are being daily transformed by the 'renewing of our mind' as we let the Lord Jesus flood every area of our lives.

Over the last few years our family has suffered much personal stress. We decided that we had to make a radical change in our lives. The obvious choice to many would have been to let go of home education. We considered this briefly and decided that it was not an option. Once again after much prayer and consideration we felt that the Lord was showing us a different route. Mark was able to leave the computer industry in order to take a sabbatical year and to re-train so that he can undertake a more home based profession and lifestyle.

Through years discipling our own sons, Mark has gained a passion to raise men of God and to this end he has been able to develop material and run a course entitled Biblical Manhood. I find that as I get older, my desire is to be in line with the older woman of Titus 2 who is exhorted to teach younger women to 'love their husbands, love their children and be homemakers', amongst other things. Far from sapping us of all our strength, home education has stretched our personalities and increased our passion for God.

Our youngest child is only five and we anticipate many more years of home education but for now it seems as though things have come full circle back to Mark's original vision for us as young Christians preparing for marriage and family life. We have kept our children close by our sides, teaching them in the ways of the Lord as we go about our daily lives as instructed in Deuteronomy 6:7. Judging from the sixth form tutor's comments we have indeed found 'the best school' for our children and we look forward to many more exciting times as we seek to follow God's path.

Portrait of a Home Educating Family

- Alan and Elspeth Bright
- Children – five boys and one girl
- Age range between nine and twenty
- Living in East London
- Have home educated for fifteen years

> If we don't create for our children a God-focused environment then the secular/pagan environment in which we allow them to be immersed will seduce them from the Truth.

This quote appeared in a Christian magazine a few years ago. It was in the context of Christian schools, but how much more does this apply to home education.

About us

We – Alan and Elspeth Bright – live, with our six children, in East London. The children's ages range from nine to twenty. Our house is not large (around 900 square feet) but the mortgage has been small.

Alan has been in full-time employment outside the home for most of our married life, mostly in the City. He is out of the house from 7.15 AM each day but unimportant enough to be home soon after six o'clock each evening. Elspeth is at home with the children. We are both university graduates,

Alan in banking and international finance and Elspeth in optometry.

We have been home educating for fifteen years. Our four oldest children went to nurseries for five mornings a week and then they came home full-time when they were five years old. Our oldest two children took GCSEs from home and then attended a local sixth form college.

How it started

Home education appeared on our radar when our oldest child was four. We were talking to some American friends whose oldest child was the same age. They told us that they intended teaching him at home. We can remember how surprised we were; after all, when you are five you go to school. *We* did and that was what our children were going to do – weren't they?

Perhaps not. We spent the next year looking into home education. We met other families who were already home educating and read lots of books. Two authors who influenced us were Mary Pride and John Holt. Then, when it was time for our oldest child to start formal education, full-time at school . . . we simply kept him at home.

What we do

Education has mostly been based around the three Rs, Scripture and foreign languages, with science and history popping up most days. Of course, teachable moments can arise at any time, and we try to be sensitive to such opportunities.

The daily routine starts with breakfast around 8.30 AM, Alan having left for work over an hour before. After breakfast come household jobs such as vacuuming, cleaning the toilets and musical instrument practice and 'school' lasts until around 12.30 PM, with a mid-morning break.

Schoolwork generally takes place at the kitchen table – the only table in the house – although children can be found working all over the house including in their bedrooms, in the living room, and in the garden in the summer.

The afternoons are varied but include visits to parks, meeting other home educating families and music lessons. Towards the end of the afternoon there are various activities with 'schooled' children such as dancing, drama, Cubs and swimming lessons.

Curricula

Curricula we have used include The Weaver (Alpha Omega), Konos and Sonlight. We have found these a little restrictive but did discover from them what we wanted to do, and what seemed to suit our children. We now tend to pick and choose from a wide variety of sources; including Saxon and Singapore for maths (we have also used Ginn and SPMG – both British). For science we have used Considering God's Creation, A Beka Book and various Dorling Kindersley publications for home-spun unit studies. History and geography have been tackled mostly using the literature approach, (Sonlight is very good for getting started on this technique) using whatever resources we have had to hand. Television programmes can be carefully chosen to fit in with whatever we've been doing, but we now rarely watch schools' programmes, finding them too simple. We tend to watch documentaries in the evenings.

Our methods have changed over the years according to the ages and learning styles of our children. The Sonlight curriculum has probably suited us best since it involves reading real books, not textbooks. All our children have responded very well to this method, and we have followed several years' worth of the curriculum. Alan has taken the older children through Sonlight's *20th Century World History* – which we have found very good.

We rarely test our children to see how they are doing. We have many friends whose children are at school and it is therefore tempting to wonder how they compare (and incidentally, they are doing fine). Just about the only regular test we have is a very simple reading one (Holborn Reading Scale). We have tended to use this only on the children we knew were doing well, purely to boost our confidence.

Taking a year out

In 1997, when our oldest son Richard reached secondary school age, we sent him to St Edward's – a Church of England secondary school. St Edward's takes children from homes only where there is significant parental involvement in church. Richard did have an enjoyable year at school but decided that he would prefer to stay at home, given that travel to school took up so much time (an hour each way). If the school had been next door we might have been less inclined to continue home educating him through the secondary years.

Bringing Richard back home was quite daunting. It is often said that the bravest home educators are those who take their children out of school – that is a far more difficult decision to take than not sending them to school in the first place. Richard being at home did mean more work for us, but there are also all the small but cumulative advantages of home education – for example, no looking for clean trousers at 6.45 AM, not having to organise bus fares and packed lunches, no 'Have you done your homework yet?', no money needed for school trips – and so on.

GCSEs

Taking GCSEs from home seemed challenging. Parents who had done it told us that they had muddled through somehow – and that is what seems to have happened for us. Our oldest two children, the only ones to have reached this stage so far, both took five subjects.

Our Local Education Authority (the London Borough of Newham) inspects us once every eighteen months or so. After each meeting they have said things along the lines of 'anything we can do to help'. So, we took the initiative and asked them to find a local school where our sons could sit GCSEs as external candidates.

It took some time, but eventually they came back with schools for us to contact. We did so and the teachers proved very helpful in terms of exam technique, past papers and coursework. Indeed, it has been quite humbling to realise that they have been spending all this time on us. Also the cost has been only £25 per GCSE.

Support

We are members of Education Otherwise (E.O.), '. . . which provides support and information for families whose children are being educated outside school, and for those who wish to uphold the freedom of families to take proper responsibility for the education of their children'. E.O. publishes a bi-monthly newsletter, to which we have contributed articles, and has some thriving local groups. We have not joined in with these groups mainly because of pressure of time. However, we feel that it is worth being part of E.O. so that there is an organisation speaking with a single voice for those educating their children outside the school system.

We are also members of the Home Service, a national support organisation, specifically for Christians who home educate. It has a list of contacts and has established the first national UK telephone support service for Christian home educators.

We have attended national conferences organised by the Home Service and have ourselves run small conferences in East London. We draw on members of the Home Service for support, encouragement and swapping ideas. Some of this has been via telephone and email, with less face-to-face contact.

There is another home educating family at our church, from whom we gain support and there are also other Christian home educators who live within two or three miles of our home. We have put on plays together and shared facilities for physical education.

The best things about home educating

Home education keeps the family together. Our older children have been able to continue doing things with us as a family. This covers leisure activities but also household chores, without us being concerned that we are asking too much of them on top of a long school day and homework.

We know more about our children. We know them, we know how they are doing and we can adapt our approach accordingly. They are also learning by being together, watching each other's needs being cared for, seeing how to look after babies and younger children and realising the consequences of not doing your job when no one else has the time to do it for you.

Can anybody do it?

Home education is part of a seamless robe. If the children are not used to obeying their parents then home education will be a hard slog. Also, there are some specialist skills needed on the part of the parent(s) as teacher, which become more important as the child grows. For us these have included maths and modern languages. In our opinion, it is easy to see how a parent not too confident in maths would find it difficult to deliver a quality education in the subject, as the children got older. Of course, some home educators use outside paid help for specialist subjects.

The greatest problems in home educating

For Alan, early on, it was the criticism from others, especially respected Christian friends. Alan suspects this is because we challenged their ways of life (few children; one and a half incomes, if not two; the slightly embarrassed search for 'the good school'). This in turn can lead to him having a wrong attitude, being judgmental and with feelings of superiority towards fellow believers.

For Elspeth there are different problems since it is she who has to deliver most of the teaching. There is the constant struggle of juggling the demands of six children all in the house at once. There are the questions at supermarket checkouts, 'No school today?' which should be a chance to fly the flag for home education but which, depending on how the day has gone, can be tedious. The children are usually briefed well before the checkout/bus queue/doctor's surgery on whether to give the economical-with-the-truth answer or the 'Hey, we're home educated' answer!

Summary

We have found home educating to be an exciting challenge. It has given us a life less ordinary and does contribute positively to the family. It has freed us in so many ways, but we do not want to give the impression that everything is easy and that our children are turning out as spiritual giants. Our family life has not been as easy as some of the books on home education might seem to indicate – but perhaps that is because we read and remember only the bits we want to. Also, we as parents can be lukewarm and sinful. But we are thankful to God for having led us on this path.

Our Home Schooling Journey

- Chris and Julie Okpoti
- Children – two boys and one girl
- Age range between two and nine
- Living in Lancashire
- Have home educated for nine years

We were blessed with our first bundle of joy, Rebekah, in 1993 and life has never been the same since! She was such a gift to us as we had waited five years for her arrival, with much prayer and petitioning to the Lord. We had our baby without thinking 'education'. However, the question of education was soon upon us. The first awareness came at the toddler group where the other mothers were talking of where their little one was going next and where they had put their son or daughter's name down for playgroup or reception class. I was asked the dreaded question, 'Which playgroup is Rebekah going to?' About the same time we received a letter from the local authority saying Rebekah's name had been put down at our local school and would we like to go and visit. We were amazed, as we had not made any approach to the school! We did pay a visit but there was a growing conviction in our hearts that we were to bring up our child in God's ways, to honour the Lord, and for her to be trained in and by the Lord. We had not waited five years for our daughter just to hand her over to a secular humanistic system of teaching.

We were really being challenged by God. We were two committed Christians, serving the Lord in church, in work and in our community, having to make such an important decision about the education and spiritual growth and feeding of our child. Should we place her in an environment where there would be little knowledge and love of our Saviour? We just couldn't do it.

The Lord had already challenged me about my return to work when Rebekah was one year old. After six months maternity leave I had gone back to work for six months but within that time the Lord led us clearly. I resigned from my career of fifteen years in the insurance industry to be a wife, homemaker and a stay-at-home mum. It wasn't without a struggle on my part. I felt I was giving up what I had worked for for all those years and, although the rewards of being at home were great, those feelings and emotions were very real at the time. So we gained the victory through obedience as is ever the way with the Lord. There is always a cost or sacrifice required on our part when we need to do the right thing before God. Rebekah did go to a playgroup two mornings a week where we knew all the staff were Christians.

Meanwhile, we were praying, 'Lord, direct us; what is your will for Rebekah?' We had never heard of home schooling or Christian education but we believed that as you seek then you will find. We had recently moved to a new place of worship and there we met a family of home schoolers. This was very exciting for us. We went to visit them at home, spent a 'typical' day with them and saw the curriculum they used. They were educating their five children at that time, using the ACE (Accelerated Christian Education) programme. We followed this visit by contacting TEACH – The European Academy for Christian Home Schooling – although it wasn't called TEACH in those days. They sent us their prospectus to look over. TEACH was set up to assist parents with the biblical and God-given task of bringing up their own children in the fear and admonition of the Lord and preparing them for the purpose God has for their lives. We had, by this time, learned that there were Christian schools in our area using this same curriculum. We contacted two of the schools and paid a visit to each. The members of staff were very welcoming and we gained much information. Whilst gleaning, we were praying all the while.

The Lord gave us a number of Scriptures which we knew, by faith, were God's answer to us in the way that we should go. These included:

> Love the Lord your God with all your heart and with all your soul and with all your strength. These commandments that I give you today are to be upon your hearts. Impress them on your children. Talk about them when you sit at home and when you walk along the road, when you lie down and when you get up. Tie them as symbols on your hands and bind them on your foreheads. Write them on the doorframes of your houses and on your gates. (Deuteronomy 6:5–9)

> Train a child in the way he should go, and when he is old he will not turn from it. (Proverbs 22:6)

> See to it that no one takes you captive through hollow and deceptive philosophy, which depends on human tradition and the basic principles of this world rather than on Christ. (Colossians 2:8)

We had our answer and both of us agreed that home schooling, not a Christian school, was the way forward. It was so important that we sought the Lord on this matter, that he answered and that we, as husband and wife, were in agreement. As we agreed together and with the Lord, that unity brought God's blessing. At those moments in our lives when we are asking, 'What next for our child?' it is important that we seek the Lord. He has promised that, if we seek him, we will find his answer for our family. There is no greater gift than salvation for each child. We, as parents, have our part to play by our example lived out before our children and in providing an education based on the Word of God and the principles laid down in it.

We registered with TEACH and went through their training package. I was so blessed by this training, my spirit just kept on saying, 'Yes, yes, yes, I want this for our child'. I read their Philosophy of Education; the Five Laws of Learning; discipline at home and good parenting; the structure of Paces (workbooks); learning that was precept upon precept; how I as parent was to supervise the work; how children would learn to set their own goals; achieve those same goals; be given responsibility and trust to score and check their own work as part of the learning procedure. Each Pace had a verse from Scripture to memorise and a character trait to learn and emulate. Paces were structured for mastery learning and repeat Paces were available. I also learned that rewards and credits helped motivation. This was an individualised and non-graded programme for Rebekah to work at her own level of achievement and pace; a programme which could take her through from pre-school to college or university; a programme accepted by the ICCE (The International Certificate of Christian Education) Board.

I am a practical person and making the decision to home educate was one thing, but working out how to go about it was daunting. This curriculum was absolutely God-sent for us. I like some structure; I needed to know where I was going. The scope and sequence aid provided showed me the content of each Pace and how they were ordered sequentially.

I completed the training with TEACH and started Rebekah right at the very beginning on the pre-school programme. Isaac came along in 1998 and three years later he started on the pre-school programme. Josiah was born in 2000 and never needed pre-schooling as he did not live long but was 'promoted to heaven', to be with the Lord. Now we have Michael. He is due to start pre-school in another year, God willing. So you see this programme has served us well these past nine years. But I do appreciate that maybe this type of structure does not suit everyone. Parents need to ask themselves some searching questions, know themselves, what type of person they are, what they will be able to realistically sustain, to settle on the right curriculum for their family and to avoid unnecessary disappointments. Looking at a number of Christian curricula before starting; gathering as much information as possible from other home schoolers, resource days, books, websites and prospectuses, is all helpful. Parents need to make an informed, God directed choice, ensuring that whatever curriculum they select, the educational needs of their child are being met.

It was 1997, Rebekah was settling in well with her Paces and little routine of bookwork in the mornings, with plenty of breaks, and other family activities, play and rest in the afternoons. I had a call; my mother was not well. She was a widow, lived alone and had been rushed into hospital. The diagnosis was bad; it was cancer. With some treatment, chemotherapy and radiotherapy to help the symptoms the prognosis gave her only six months to live! She was fifty-four years old. Rebekah and her grandmother had a wonderful relationship. They saw each other often as we were only forty minutes drive away. We now had a choice before us. Mum wanted to be at home but she needed care. My brother worked. I was the one at home, but what about Rebekah? We prayed; for healing, for understanding and wisdom, for strength. There are times when you have to pray as you go. I went with Rebekah to live at Grandma's for those precious, last six months. Grandma saw her granddaughter every day. First thing in the morning Rebekah was there playing with her grandma at her bedside. She was a joy to my mother through those days and Rebekah has the memory of that time with her grandmother. I prayed, 'Lord, are you going to heal my mother? I need to know.' His answer was very clear, 'Yes, in heaven.' The Lord always knows what is in the future, what will come into our lives, the joys and the sorrows. I thanked the Lord Jesus then and still do that he led us to home school, to a structured curriculum that actually gave us a flexibility to pack up and, with my husband's blessing, go and care for my mother in her own home, literally until her dying day. When we packed our clothes to stay at Grandma's house, we also packed Rebekah's workbooks so that her little routine of bookwork in the mornings, whilst spending time with Grandma, could continue.

There was continuity in Rebekah's 'education'. Why do I say 'education', for what is education really? Someone once defined education as what is left when you have forgotten everything you have learned. Rebekah and I had lessons of life over those six months, made possible not by keeping Rebekah away from her grandmother but by bringing the two of them closer together. Rebekah saw how to care for her grandma and met many health visitors and professionals who were interested in our home schooling. There were many opportunities to share why we were home schooling and openings to testify to our love for the Lord Jesus Christ. The choice for me was just to go, not , 'Do I stay because my child is in school?' or, 'What will she miss if she's taken out of school?' It was not a choice between my daughter and my mother; I could be with both and meet both their different, individual needs at the same time. I praise God. What a loving Father we have who arranges that 'all things work together for good'.

My mother was a Christian and when Rebekah went into her room one morning the bed was neatly made. Rebekah asked, 'Where is Grandma?' I sat her on the bed and told her that Jesus had come in the night and taken Grandma to live with him. In a typical child's response she said, 'Did she have time to pack?' Our children lead us grown-ups at times in their acceptance and faith. Home schooling was a blessing to me through that time and the more I journey on this Christian home schooling path, the more I see and receive the blessings and benefits.

Not that it is always plain sailing. We all have our good days and our bad days. When those bad days come, we have to be honest, recognise them for what they are and say tomorrow will be a better day, then we will start a new page because we know that God's mercies are new every morning. We have days when one child is ill which takes Mum's or Dad's attention, or the unannounced visitor comes calling, or the work is just too difficult and much more one-to-one time is needed; the new baby comes home, or breastfeeding is not going so well. There is always a pile of ironing, cooking and cleaning to do; demands, demands, demands. We have to be flexible when necessary, but that does not mean undisciplined; there is a difference. For us the key is to commit our day and each family member to the Lord. It is his day whatever happens, 'This is the day the Lord has made; let us rejoice and be glad in it' (Psalm 118:24). We put family devotions into practice every day, learning from The Book before picking up any other book.

In 1998, our second child, Isaac, started on the ACE (Accelerated Christian Education) programme. Then in 2000, the Lord blessed us with Josiah, our second son. Now all home schooling families know that when there is a new arrival in the family, that term must major on child care issues. Our term of summer 2000 went a little differently. So differently, in fact, that schooling stopped completely. Josiah was born full-term but with Edwards' syndrome (a trisomy 18 baby); his life expectancy was only weeks. We brought Josiah home, loved him, prayed for him, tube-fed him breast milk and got to know him. It was more important in those few weeks for the children just to be; to be together, to be themselves, to be with Josiah. He did not stay in hospital because of the possibility that he might die at any time, and because the other children were not in school they did not miss that significant time with him. We made the most of all the time the Lord gave us and Rebekah and Isaac got to know their brother.

The doctors asked us how we felt; we answered with a verse, 'Hope deferred makes the heart sick, but a longing fulfilled is a tree of life' (Proverbs 13:12). We felt as a family that we were right in the middle of that verse. But God in his sovereign will did not leave us there and we were looking to 'a tree of life'. We should never be afraid to stop what we are doing, change it if it isn't working, have the courage of our convictions and find a way to train our children under God, whatever the circumstances of life. It is all right to stop, take a break, take time to think and reassess what we are doing. Otherwise we carry on with our heads down dealing with the daily tasks before us and we do not see the bigger picture. Husbands can be brilliant at lifting their wives' heads. They follow a good example for we know that Jesus is the lifter of our heads. It can be hard for husbands when they are out at work all day, missing the children and wanting to be more involved. Husband and wife are in this together for the long haul and the role of father as spiritual leader, breadwinner, encourager, supporter and visionary is vital.

So where are we now? Rebekah is aged twelve. She is growing into a young lady, very tall and even taller in her ballet point shoes! She has taken her grade five piano exam and her grade four violin exam with the Associated Board. She is enjoying playing in a new orchestra and enters various music festivals. She swims, reads and likes cross-stitch; she also enjoys her computer, Kids' Church and Postal Bible School. Her ACE studies are going well and she has taken on a new IT curriculum called Future Kids, to improve her computer skills. One of her hobbies is card making and she has sold many cards to raise funds for various charities. Isaac is a typical boy, seven years old, forever up trees, in the garden, dirty hands, pockets full of sand, stones, beetles, bottle tops and whatever else he may find. He has discovered Lego in a big way and his creativity has moved from plasticine into Lego, the results being some brilliant spaceships! He also plays the violin and the bongos. He and his sister have a small repertoire of duets. He enjoys swimming, Kids' Church, Postal Bible School and play tumbles with his brother, Michael. Isaac is always talking and asking questions which is great because, although we use ACE, we like to take the lesson off the page and bring in other helpful aids which Isaac can relate to. So, for example, when the Science Pace teaches about reptiles shedding their skin, we go to a friend's house to see their snake and its shed skin. Geography is done by way of overseas visitors. We usually have missionaries staying with us or overseas students boarding, so we ask them to do a project with the children on their country or adopted country. The children get to know the person well and then always relate the country with that person and their time together.

Just because something has been taught does not mean it has been learnt. We teach the same lesson in a number of ways or at least reinforce when the opportunity arises. Our family have days out, excursions, even our holidays are all opportunities for learning and reinforcing. We make an excursion file for each year and any brochures, work done and photographs related to an outing are all filed. This is great fun but also very useful when the local authority inspection time comes. We just pull out that year's excursion file as evidence of trips and projects. This has not happened overnight though. Just to get up, dress, eat, do chores, do Pace work, and arrive at lunch time was enough at the beginning. These projects have developed in our family over our nine years of home schooling.

I have not told you much about Michael. Michael is the baby of our family, two years old. He likes to play a lot at home, enjoys toddler group at church and chatting away, even though we grown ups don't always catch his meaning. Michael is so special to us; he is our adopted son. We are foster parents for our local authority and Michael was placed with us over a year ago. It became apparent that Michael would need a 'for ever' family and we were approved as his adoptive parents. We are grateful to the Lord Jesus for allowing us to be a part of Michael's life and for bringing him into our family. His adoption has taught us much about our relationship with our heavenly Father and how we, as Christians, are adopted into the family of God. 2 Corinthians 6:18 says, 'I will be a Father to you, and you will be my sons and daughters, says the Lord Almighty'.

When Jesus was asked, 'What is the greatest commandment?' He replied, 'Love the Lord your God with all your heart, and with all your soul, and with all your mind'. This is what he wants us to diligently teach our children. We need to give our children a Bible-based, Christ-honouring education that will lead them to love the Lord our God and bring glory to his Name.

Home School Adventure, Allcock Style

- Graham and Pauline Allcock
- Children – one boy and one girl
- Aged fourteen and fifteen
- Living in West Yorkshire
- Have home educated for nine years

We started home schooling at the end of May 1997 when our daughter Lynette was aged six and a half and our son Stephen had just turned five. Lynette had been in school for one year and two terms and Stephen just two terms. Graham was nursing at the time but eight months later entered church pastoral ministry. Home schooling has proved a real blessing with the number of house moves we have had to undertake in the last eight years, as we have not had to worry about trying to find the 'good' schools in the towns where we've lived!

Our reasons

These were many and varied but included the following:

- To fulfil our responsibility as Christian parents in the light of Proverbs 22:6 and Deuteronomy 6,
- Freedom for our children to develop and progress at their own pace and ability,

- Concerns over the content of the National Curriculum and school life as a whole,
- Freedom to set our own hours, timetable, curriculum and holidays,
- To develop and maintain a fuller relationship with our children.

Getting started

We approached the head teacher and told her of our decision to give our children a home-based education. She was very understanding and said we were fully entitled to do what we thought was best for our children. She contacted our Local Education Authority (LEA) and found out what we needed to do to deregister the children.

During the primary years we approached our studies mainly in a topical way and found our local library had plenty of good resources. We linked our studies to what was happening in our lives, such events as moving house, learning about Egypt when Graham went on a three week evangelistic trip there, and doing a project on the railways during the 125th anniversary celebrations, when we lived in Darlington.

Home education has been a real blessing to our family. There have been many joys, but like all aspects of life, some real challenges as well.

Joys

- As parents, being able to have a meaningful private devotional time in the morning before coming together for family worship, without having to keep watching the clock thinking it's time to rush off to school!
- To see the children developing spiritually as well as academically.

- To be able to be involved in the process of Stephen learning to read. My daughter learnt to read largely at school but I had a real kick out of seeing Stephen progress with his reading. To me, it was on a par with seeing him take his first steps as a baby.
- Having a close relationship with our children, especially when we see so many teenagers who do not experience this closeness in their own family situations.

Challenges

- To find ways of explaining something in simpler terms when the children are not grasping what I am trying to teach them. I have to keep reminding myself (or the children remind me) that I have the advantage of knowing things as an adult and they are coming to it for the first time. This particularly applies in maths!
- To find some time for myself to do those things which I need to do or which I would like to do.
- To balance my time so that each child gets a fair (not necessarily equal) share of my time, bearing in mind their different abilities and learning styles.
- To help my son not to feel inferior and stop him from comparing himself with his sister and her abilities.
- In the early days having patience to allow them to help me with the cooking, when I could do it much quicker myself! This is not such a challenge any longer as their culinary skills are such that they no longer require so much supervision in the kitchen and can turn out some lovely meals.

Reactions

Reactions to our decision to take the children out of school were mixed, with the number one question relating to socialisation. My way of dealing with this was to ask the person concerned what they meant by socialisation. I also pointed out to them that by the end of Stephen's first week at school, he proudly announced that he had learned to 'push and shove' (his own words) in order to hang his coat up. He went on to explain that he did this because the dinner ladies were hassling him to hang his coat up and then to go and sit on the carpet in the classroom. So, rather than stand back as I had instructed him to do, he obeyed the dinner ladies, copied the other children and pushed and shoved until his coat was hung up – not the type of social skills I wanted him to learn!

Another reaction concerned the fact that I had spent many years studying law and I was now 'wasting' those years of study by not returning to employment now the children were of school age. (I had made the decision before we were married that I would raise my own children and so had not worked since they were born.) Others actually expressed admiration and respect that I would be willing to give up my own career prospects to teach my children at home. I was convinced that my children's spiritual and social well-being were far more important than any career, so it was not such a difficult decision to make.

There were some, especially within the church, who implied (not always in so many words) that I was perhaps trying to make them feel guilty because they were not willing to home school their children. I dealt with this by making it clear that we were doing what we felt the Lord was calling us to do and that each parent has the responsibility to decide what is best for them and their own children. I pointed out that for the majority of parents, they were completely unaware that school was not compulsory and just sent their children off to school without considering or realising there were other options.

Contact with the Local Education Authority (LEA)

A week after seeing the school head teacher and telling her of our plans to home school the children, we received a letter from our LEA. They were asking for details of the arrangements we intended to make, including details of the educational programme and the curriculum we intended to provide, together with details of timetable, resources, teaching and so on. This was before we had even formally written to the head teacher informing her of our decision to remove the children from school!

I felt a bit intimidated by the letter from the LEA but contacted some other experienced home schoolers who assured me that I was not under any obligation to provide all the information the LEA was requesting. I therefore wrote back saying we intended to cover such subjects as English, maths, science, geography, history, technology, music, art, physical education and religious education and would deal with this mainly in a topical way, rather than in separate subjects.

A month after taking the children out of school, we received a letter from a Specialist Advisor at the area education office, asking to arrange a visit to discuss our children's education. The visit went very well and the advisor was quite impressed with the range of resources we had already acquired. She tried to stress that it would be sensible for us to follow the National Curriculum and familiarise ourselves with its expectations at each Key Stage. We diplomatically chose not to get into a debate about the pros and cons of the National Curriculum and expecting all children to be at the same level just because they were the same age. We didn't hear anything further from the LEA.

The following year we moved to another town. I wrote to the LEA stating that we had recently moved into the area and intended to continue to home school our children. I subsequently found out that we were in fact under no obligation to contact the LEA at all and later I came to wish that I hadn't!

This LEA was obviously not as familiar with the principle of home schooling as the previous one was and we had a letter from them asking us to submit a programme/timetable of education. They said they would then arrange for a home visit from a member of the advisory team. Various phone calls and letters followed in which staff from the LEA kept asking for timetables and the like and I kept telling them we were under no obligation to provide this information. It was at this time I came across a book in our local library entitled *School is Not Compulsory*, produced by Education Otherwise and this was extremely helpful in my further dealings with the LEA. I eventually produced a letter (based on an example in the book), which seemed to satisfy the education department and they simply arranged for a home visit.

After all the telephone calls and letters we were not quite sure what to expect when the advisor came. However, she was very friendly and told us that it was the policy of the LEA to have minimal involvement, once they knew that the children were in fact being educated and were not just playing all day! She did not ask to see any of the children's work. She just chatted to us generally and asked if I would be willing to let the children read to her. I said it was up to the children and they agreed and read to her a little bit each. She seemed quite satisfied and said that she felt that we were providing an adequate education and the children were obviously happy and contented.

A few days later we received a letter from her confirming that she was satisfied that we were providing appropriate education for the children. She went on to say that as our time in the town was likely to be relatively short, she would not plan a return visit but that we were free to contact her any time, should we have questions or want advice.

I have chosen not to contact the LEAs in the towns where we have since moved.

Curriculum

We have not followed any particular curriculum but have used various resources, including work books from Schofield and Sims, Letts, and Coordination Group Publishers (CGP). These have all been easily obtainable from bookshops and libraries.

Now that the children are older, we have purchased a maths package for the computer from Maths 2XL, which covers Key Stages 3 and 4 of the National Curriculum. This provides a personal tutorial style of lesson with worksheets to print out. The completed answers are then entered into the computer which marks the child's work and shows the solutions, should the child get the question wrong and not be able to see where they have made a mistake.

We have struggled somewhat in finding good science resources for secondary level. My school science classes were short lived and therefore I feel rather inadequate when it comes to teaching science. We are currently going through Dr Jay Wile's *Exploring Creation through General Science*. My daughter enjoys this more than my son. We have found the text to be rather repetitious, although on the whole it is set out well, with items for the experiments being easily obtainable.

We have enjoyed reading science biographies including *The Story of Thomas Edison* by Margaret Cousins and *Isaac Newton* by John Hudson Tiner. We are currently reading through *The Story of Inventions* by Michael McHugh.

Lynette is teaching herself German, with the use of a Linguaphone package.

We have made use of Chris Eastwood's *History Notes of Britain*, along with other historical resources such as videos my parents have recorded for the children about what the Romans and the Tudors taught us. We have enjoyed visits to places of historical interest, such as Housesteads Fort on Hadrian's Wall, and hearing all about the terrible working conditions children faced in the cotton mill industry, on our visit to the Manchester Museum of Science and Industry. We have visited many museums over the years.

Both children have music lessons, Lynette is learning to play the piano and Stephen the trumpet.

Financial implications

Obviously, having made the choice to home school my children, it means that I cannot have a regular job that brings in a second wage. With the hours that my husband works I cannot even have a regular part-time job, so finances are rather tight, but God has been good and we have many reasons to praise him.

Concluding remarks

Nine years on, we have not regretted our decision to home school our children. At the outset we did not set any time limit on how long we would continue to provide a home based education but instead said we would let the Lord guide us, and he has. There are some things we would do differently if we could turn the clock back but on the whole we feel the children have received a very broad based education. We have also had many people say that the children are 'a credit' to us, although we have pointed out that this is not our own doing but as a result of God's grace in their lives and ours. We are not a perfect family and we all have our off-days but we would certainly recommend home schooling to other families on the basis that the joys far outweigh the challenges.

Life and Learning
with Lots of Little Ones

- Mike and Anne Kitchen
- Children – three boys and two girls
- Age range between two and nine years
- Living in the Wirral
- Have always home educated

Our short home school history is one of change and challenge. I sometimes think that a bit of routine and stability would be appreciated but I can't deny that I like a challenge! The Lord has given us the opportunity to home school five children so far. Our eldest had just turned seven when our fifth child was born.

Let me introduce the Kitchen family. Mike became a nurse in 2000 after being a carpenter for many years and then retraining. I gained a French degree in 1992 and then worked in a shop and an office. I only used my degree after the birth of our first child, when the Lord provided a job as a private French tutor in an infant school. Mike was a student nurse at the time, and although I didn't want to work outside our home, my wage from this job kept us from going hungry!

In August 1997 we were blessed with our first child – Asher. Callum was born seventeen months later on New Year's Day in 1999. Then our third son arrived in July 2001. Benjamin was followed seventeen months later by our first daughter Rosanna who arrived on Christmas Eve 2002. Then in September 2004 we were delighted by the arrival of Serena Grace. We hoped she would be serene and we knew we would need a lot of grace with the arrival of a fifth child!

Why we home educate

I love teaching. I have never been trained to teach but I love the challenge of finding the right way to explain something, so that a particular child can not only understand it but can see the beauty in it and find joy in knowing it. I started teaching piano at the age of fourteen.

The first time I came across the fact that it was actually possible to home educate in Britain was when I saw an article in *Good Housekeeping* magazine. It appealed to me immediately and, even though I was still single at the time, I decided I would home educate if I ever had children!

Mike hated school. He was bullied in primary school in Portsmouth. Then his family moved to Wales when he was twelve and as an English boy in a Welsh school he found it was difficult to fit in. Not only did he not speak Welsh, but he liked football instead of rugby!

How we started

We started networking with home educators even while Asher and Callum were toddlers. We were glad for this opportunity to make friends and to read around the subject. We went to home schooling conferences whenever we could and we found the fellowship and support very encouraging.

We didn't set a schedule for 'school' in the early days. Learning just happened naturally and we just did what suited us at the time. We read loads of books and visited the library as often as we could. We walked in the park and talked about the changing seasons. We played with other children from home educated families when possible. We were fortunate that there were three other families home educating in our area at the time. They all had children of similar ages to our three boys.

Reading and writing

I was very keen for Asher to start reading. When he had just turned four, I looked around for a reading programme and found a book called *Teach Your Child to Read in 100 Easy Lessons*. Anything that had 'easy' in the title appealed to me, because I had never done this before! I ordered the book from Amazon and it worked. By the age of four and a half Asher was reading. He just loved being able to read and he read everything – even the labels on food. He asked us one day why a bottle of sauce contained 1.6 megahertz of sodium!

Mike devised a game to encourage the children's maths skills. Asher and Callum both had to roll a die across the floor twice and add their scores together. Whoever rolled the highest number got to pick a Bible story. I didn't worry about following a maths curriculum as this game created a sense of fun about maths and both the boys showed a familiarity with numbers that was more than acceptable for their age.

We played a lot, baked a lot and had a lot of visitors. We felt our lives were rich with educational opportunities. We kept a world map in the kitchen and talked about different places our visitors were from or had been to. We didn't follow a set curriculum but simply answered the children's many, many questions.

It seemed no time at all until Callum was four and I started teaching reading for the second time. I used . . . *100 Easy Lessons* again as it had worked so well the first time. It was easier for me the second time, as I was more familiar with the whole process, although it was frustrating at times because Callum sometimes has difficulty hearing. Even though he was sitting on my lap or right next to me, he couldn't catch the sounds properly and we didn't realise that there was a problem with his hearing for quite some time. Although he occasionally mixed up some sounds, he was reading well by the age of five. Once we realised that he couldn't always hear very well, we made allowance for it, and things became easier. We were very glad at this point that he was being taught at home, because he would probably have day-dreamed his way through the first couple of years at school and no doubt would have been labelled in some way, possi-bly to his detriment. Now he is a confident seven-year-old with a reading age well above his years. I think that if he had been at school and lost in a sea of thirty or so children, he probably wouldn't be reading at all, even now.

I am presently using . . . *100 Easy Lessons* for the third time, with Benjamin. I am so glad I bought the book four years ago and pleased it has worked for us. I know some parents who have found it hasn't worked for them. However, it teaches reading through synthetic phonics and research has shown that children who learn synthetic phonics continue to advance in their reading after they have finished their reading programme. I have found this to be the case. Both our older sons now read well above their age or grade level. They love reading and they read constantly without anyone telling them to do so. The authors state that the book is actu-ally a tool to start a child reading, and that children will need some assistance to continue to put into practice what they have learnt, once they have finished the book. After a few weeks of extra practice using some easy readers, the boys took off, reading by themselves.

. . . *100 Easy Lessons* also includes learning to write. After each lesson, which generally lasts about twenty minutes, the child has to copy two sounds which you write down for them. This is quite elementary, so I followed it up with the Getty Dubay handwriting books. As I had been told (and have now discovered for myself!) that most boys dislike unnecessary writing, I have tried to minimise the amount of writing required. I think most writing required in schools is only necessary because the teacher is so busy. We have done lots of mental maths and even now sometimes I let Callum tell me the answers to his maths questions. I simply write 'completed orally' and the date it was done in his maths book.

Teaching with babies and toddlers

As our children are so close in age, I have been either pregnant or breastfeeding for most of the past eight years. I have found it very difficult to cope with broken nights and then early mornings in order to start school at 9.00 AM. Also, Mike works shifts, so he sometimes comes home for dinner at 10.00 PM. I struggle with the fact that each week is different. I love the days or weeks when we sleep well and when the chores are done before breakfast, but they don't happen often enough! I have had to learn to be much more flexible than I would naturally be.

We have an outline schedule now for the two older boys, but when they were all under six, it was impossible to keep to a schedule. Even now, our day is based around the three daily meals, and chores are usually done either before or after meals. Most academic work is done in the mornings, and we have music on Tuesday afternoons and art on Wednesday afternoons. We try to go swimming on Mondays and we try to practise some tennis as well, maybe every two weeks or so.

When we just had the three boys, we did several unit studies. I created these myself using tips from *How to Create Your Own Unit Study* by Valerie Bendt. I think the boys' favourite was The Solar System. They still talk about it now and Asher loves anything to do with space.

During the summer that I was pregnant with Rosanna, we did a unit study on our local park. It combined fulfilling my legal obligation to educate my children while being pregnant and looking after a baby, enjoying a pleasant summer, getting enough exercise and not going insane trying to keep three little boys tied to their seats all day!

We taught Asher and Callum how to load and unload the dishwasher. We made sure they could butter a piece of bread. Then we showed them how to slice up a banana so that the pieces of bread could become a sandwich. All of a sudden lunch could be on the table while I was still heaving my ever expanding tummy off the sofa!

It seemed like five minutes later that I was pregnant again, only this time I had two babies to look after, as well as two school-age children to teach. As I had struggled with four children aged five and under, I was actually dreading trying to manage five children with the oldest turning seven one month before the fifth was due.

Learning as a family

When all the children were small I felt that my workload was never ending, and that I would have to do all this by myself for ever. As it turned out, when I was pregnant with baby number five, we began to reap the benefits of teaching the children to help in the home. I taught Asher to make hot drinks. We added to his sandwich making abilities and we taught him to use the vacuum cleaner.

I have been very aware of the possibility of burnout over the last four years or so. I was ill when I was nineteen and suffered from exhaustion and depression. I have been determined not to allow myself to burn out again. Thankfully the Lord has preserved me, and we are grateful for good friends who have helped out at difficult times. But we have had no hesitation in cancelling school for a day or a week if necessary.

Our schedule is a guide, not a master. The children are all learning every day, whether or not we do 'school'. We are having to learn alongside the children that what matters is what God has appointed for us each day – if that means academic work one day, rest and recuperation or DIY the next, then so be it.

Mike loves teaching the children. If there is maintenance to be done in the home or on the car he often has a child or two to help. We count this as part of their education. It is one of the advantages of shift work that Mike is sometimes available in the mornings to share the load or to broaden the scope of the children's education.

Since September 2005 we have been working for four weeks and then taking a week off. It is working well so far. I am very tired after four weeks of school. Daily life is demanding enough as it is and when we are not engaged in any academic work I wonder how we do actually manage to achieve any at all, as the days are still so full!

Bible reading

I also realised that I need to focus my attention on the Word of God. There have been times when I thought I would go insane with all the demands of four and then five small children. God promises us that he will keep us in perfect peace, if our mind is stayed on him. I wanted perfect peace in my home – I often cried and yelled because we didn't have it! But the Lord showed me that what I need is the very thing that I felt was impossible – time spent reading the Word of God. A friend told me recently that the rule in their house is 'No Bible, no breakfast'. We have adopted that as our motto this year, so almost every morning I read the Bible for half an hour when I wake up. Sometimes this means that we eat breakfast at 9.30 AM, but this matters less to me than trying to get breakfast at 8.00 AM and saying that I don't have time to read the Word of God. Also I don't feel a hypocrite when I make the children wait for their breakfast until we have done our daily reading. We are currently using *Keys for Kids* as a daily devotional. Things that seem impossible when the children are small suddenly start getting easier! It was very difficult to have a family Bible reading when we only had two small children. Now that the older children are able to help with and enjoy a daily Bible reading it is becoming a habit.

Reading the Bible before breakfast means that we feel that even if we achieve nothing else all day, we have at least given the Lord his rightful place. I always felt there was something missing when we didn't do our Bible reading, but we often used to forget and it was difficult to get everyone together again once they had left the table after breakfast. Having our reading before breakfast has solved this problem. Also, doing Scripture memory straight after breakfast means that this (usually) doesn't get forgotten. We print out the memory passages and attach them to the fridge door with magnets so they are easy for the children to read each day.

Housework

Another thing that has become easier to cope with is the mess in the house. I found it very difficult to cope when I was the only one who could really clear up properly. The mess hasn't gone away – far from it! The mess multiplies right along with the number of children! But thankfully the children are growing up and are able to help to clean up. We have a Pick-up Chart, which shows which child is responsible for picking up the mess in which room. We have a chart which shows who sets and who clears the table for each meal. We also have a schedule which means that downstairs should get cleaned each week and I am planning to expand it so that upstairs will get a weekly clean as well.

Housework is part of education in our home. I can't teach my older children, look after my little ones *and* do housework, as I don't have the strength or the time to do it all, so the children have to learn to do the housework. When all the children were small, we used to do dusting together as a family. I gave all of them a rag, sprayed on some polish and off we went. As long as we were polishing together, they were all quite happy. It wasn't quite as easy to get the vacuum cleaning done as all the toys had to be put away first! It was hard work to get the oldest two boys used to helping with chores each day. It has been much easier with the other children. They have seen the older ones being praised for doing a good job, and the little ones have been eager to take on responsibilities like the big ones!

The continuing challenge

Once I had Serena, I needed to find some way of educating the children, letting the boys run-off their energy, keeping a toddler happy, as well as allowing me to sit and feed the baby. A unit study on gardening was the answer! We hired an allotment and although we didn't get a huge amount of food from our plot last year, we had a lot of fun and hard work, and learnt a little about our wonderful world as well.

This year we are trying to achieve a little more academic work. Asher is now eight and Callum is seven so they can work by themselves for longer than before. We have gathered a variety of different curricula and they are doing Singapore Maths, Learning Language Arts through Literature, music theory, piano lessons, English from the Roots Up, art courses from How Great Thou Art publications, and French. We are also doing a unit study called *Galloping the Globe* which includes lots of subjects.

Life is incredibly challenging just now. Trying to get twenty minutes without an interruption in order to do Benjamin's reading lessons seems an impossibility. Also trying to keep a three-year-old and a four-year-old occupied while Asher and Callum do their work is a constant challenge. Then Serena sometimes wants to do 'work' at the table as well as the others. We face the challenge of teaching with pre-schoolers for quite a few years yet, but no doubt these years will disappear all too quickly. I try to remember that the children won't always be small and endeavour to accept the mess, the noise and things constantly being broken! Meanwhile I am often humbled by the readiness of the children to forgive me when I make mistakes.

It is incredible how quickly the children are growing up and I am so thankful to the Lord for teaching us as parents how to live for him and for giving us children to share the journey with. Praise the Lord!

'Oh! Is it an Inset Day Today?'

- Ross and Maggie Mackenzie
- Children – two girls and two boys
- Age range between thirteen and twenty-one
- Living in Cheshire
- Have home educated for eleven years

Home education started as a conviction which became a burden, in the sense that we felt burdened to do it. The conviction was that as the children were a gift from God, the best way that we could bring them up was to give them every spiritual encouragement. This meant teaching them from a Christian viewpoint and being involved in their lives as much as possible.

Whilst we gave ourselves a year to be sure that this was indeed the right option, increasingly it became a burden. Even now I am amazed sometimes that we do home educate . . . but we have felt that it was right to continue through twelve years so far.

We started tentatively however, and not as early as we could have done. As Hannah, our eldest, approached the official date for starting school, I also had Jon aged three and a baby due two months later. I had a feeling of uncertainty and inadequacy about home educating at that point. After Jon had completed his first three years at school however we were ready to begin . . . it was a now or never feeling.

The last twelve years have been a journey of different curricula, different methods – working with other families,
working with a group Christian Education for Deeside
(CED) – different subjects and even different exams. Looking
back on the journey, we can say that God has helped us
throughout, motivating, encouraging and particularly providing help at the times when there were certain obstacles.

We (Ross and Maggie) have four children: Hannah
(twenty-one), Jon (nineteen), Josh (sixteen) and Abi (thirteen). Home education started officially in September 1993
when we took Jon out of school (Hannah came out a year
later). As the school was on the estate where we lived, it was
quite a public thing to do. When people asked us why, we
would usually say that we wanted to teach them from a
Christian viewpoint and that we liked the idea of working
together in a small family group. Although we hadn't been
keen on the school for various reasons we wanted to stress
the positives of home education rather then the negatives of
school. Reactions varied from negative; the letter from the
Education Authority, to positive; non-Christian friends on
the estate.

So that we didn't feel completely overwhelmed we gave
ourselves a year to make sure we were going in the right
direction. At first I felt quite apprehensive and different. . . .
I didn't like going out of the house before three o'clock for
fear of being interrogated. Every adult who met us always
asked the children, 'Why aren't you at school?' or queried,
'Is it an Inset day today?' It took time to build up confidence.

When considering what to do during the day, I wanted to
use something fairly structured because it gave direction. I
had read a recommendation by Susan Schaeffer Macaulay
for the Calvert School curriculum which she was using at the
time. We were fortunate enough to meet her at a conference,
where she showed us the basic instruction guide. We
ordered it, supplementing it with the maths scheme Jon had

been using at school. When Hannah joined us a year later that scheme continued with the addition of some Bob Jones University Press material for science and English. Latin and French were also added.

Work with Josh was slightly different, we had the advantage of friends at our church who were also beginning home education and their son was three days older than Josh. So began a few years of Dan coming to us one day and Josh going to them one day a week, using a Christian curriculum (by Ann Ward, from the USA) which was for their age. Later our next two children also worked together.

Work has always begun at 9.00 AM (-ish), to establish a routine. We have tended to carry on till 12 noon, (with a break at 10.30 AM). As the children have got older the day has got progressively longer. At first you wonder how you can fill the time. By the time they are in their teens you wonder how you can fit everything in, or what you can squeeze out!

Later on we came across other curricula that we used and enjoyed – Greenleaf Press History and Diana Waring material with their emphasis on a chronological view of history and particularly the Sonlight Curriculum (also from the USA), which we are still using. It fits my style, is from a Christian perspective and has brought so much wonderful, wholesome and thoughtful literature into our home. I have never found the daily plan to be a bind but have amended or extended it as necessary.

The other big influence on our home education started with a phone call. I met someone at a local church who suggested I phone another lady in her village fifteen miles away, who was also home educating. From that grew our home education group Christian Education for Deeside (CED). Starting in homes with four families, we then moved into different community centres and churches. CED has now been meeting for over ten years. Project work, singing, trips, craft, camping holidays and latterly preparation for exams have formed part of our fortnightly Fridays. At present ten families travel to Wrexham. This has obviously been a wonderful resource for friendship, information, tutoring, socialisation and support.

Work in the early years was made much easier by being in a church that was supportive. Some families there had previously taught their own children and there was one family, who were home education pioneers, whose children were much older. Jon went to them for some project work. We enjoyed practical help (a friend taking Abi out) and friends coming in for art lessons and the occasional sewing lesson. At one stage we also had the luxury of a cleaner!

A house move eight years ago led to a different church atmosphere, partly because nobody in the new place was aware that home education was a possibility and partly because 'the schools are very good round here!' In this new situation some people's comments were positive but others were quite negative. The way I dealt with this was to keep things to myself, which meant I felt quite lonely at first and not at liberty to mention things. Obviously that is where the CED group was so helpful. The other great help of course was the Home Service conferences. They were often there at just the right time to provide the stimulus and resolve for the next year. For the last two years a new family who home educate, have been coming to the church and another existing family have started too, which has meant that I can find someone to chat to here without feeling quite so weird.

We have often been asked about inspections; we only had one in the first eight years and since our move to Cheshire we have had two and the advisors have been very fair and courteous. Needless to say the longer you home educate, the less daunting the inspections become.

If only there were no exams to do! The teenage years meant that we had to struggle with how to cope with GCSEs. I think we have covered almost every exam type and method of sitting them! Initially we decided to stagger them over a couple of years and began with correspondence courses using the Open Learning Centre for GCSEs (child development, geography) and IGSCEs (biology, physics, and chemistry). IGCSEs were used for the science subjects as they do not require a practical exam. They were quite expensive but at least provided answers and phone support although in reality I would say this was at best adequate, apart from one pilot scheme with NorthStarUK. In fact we had quite a struggle with geography course work, then we met a Christian family in the same situation, but where the father had been a geography teacher! We have remained friends ever since. That was one example of God providing help to overcome a real difficulty. The other problem with correspondence courses (and with any external exams) is that you have to find a centre to take them. Sometimes I would spend whole mornings on the phone trying to find a school that would accept us. Again, through another Christian family we were given the name of a further education college to try and we were able to use them for four exam sessions. Home educators have to be persistent, bold and willing to keep on praying.

We have been fortunate recently to have a further education college nearby which has taken under sixteen-year-olds for a limited number of GCSEs. This has the advantage of being cheap and easily accessible. Because the classes were in the evening it also meant that the people taking part had a wide age range and were usually very keen to learn. They were often also very accommodating to younger students. The only drawback is that each year the college appears to be more reluctant to take the children on and have cut back on the number of courses available, both because of financial pressures. The last application had to be supported with a well reasoned letter to the vice-principal.

Our newest experience of the exam system started in the summer of 2005 when the Cambridge exam board announced they would no longer take private candidates for IGCSE and O level exams. After a lot of researching and pushing by one of our members and having found a suitable church building with a very helpful pastor and his wife, the CED group formed an exam centre to enable families to continue with these exams. This worked well for the first year and two of our children sat O levels through the centre. We are now into our second year.

What to do about A levels? At this stage we felt that it was a good time to put them into the local sixth forms because a) I felt unable to teach science subjects at this level and b) all three were professing Christians and we felt it would be appropriate for them to be in the system before they possibly moved away. Both schools (single sex) were happy to take on home educated children; they all settled well and the schools have commented on their maturity and serious attitude to work. The older two children are now at university and found no difficulty with the admission process even though they were taught at home. Now we have only one daughter left at home and I have the luxury of devoting my time to her.

So, twelve years later . . . are we glad that we made the decision to home educate? Yes, we have no regrets about the decision and I feel that I can be more positive about our choice to others and I am less concerned about 'missing out' on aspects of school, such as sport. There are some regrets about not being as relaxed as I should have been as a mum (I really need a big poster with the words of Philippians 4:6 on the wall where we work), not being a diligent enough teacher at times and not being as encouraging with the children as I should have been. But I am really thankful that God has been faithful to us in his provision and encouragement so that we have been able to continue until now.

The greatest difference in outlook for me has been to be more concerned about spiritual and character values than about academic attainment. Sometimes people who have been negative about home education have commented that things must have gone right when they see a good academic result. I have tried to explain that that is not our motive and that what people are like is far more important than how many A* passes they have. Looking back over the years, we can most certainly say that it has been and continues to be a joy to spend time with and to learn with our children.

Being Fully Involved
– A Father's Role

- Rick and Andrea Williams
- Children – five boys and one girl
- Age range between one and seventeen
- Living in Wigtownshire, Scotland
- Have home educated for nine years

Before any of our children were born we didn't give a thought as to how they would be educated. It never crossed our minds that we would do anything other than send them to a state school. Our first child, Joshua, born in 1989, spent one year at a Church of England primary school, which we had carefully selected. However, it soon became apparent that we were being squeezed out of that part of his life and we were unhappy about this. We decided to put him and our second child, Toby, born in 1990, into a small fee-paying school run by Christians in Manchester. On the whole the school was excellent and we envisaged that, unless God moved us to a different place to live, our children would remain at the school until they were eighteen. The school used the ACE (Accelerated Christian Education) curriculum which was able to take them to A level standard.

In 1997 we became aware, that God was speaking to us about home education. The only exposure of any kind we had had to this idea was Andrea's sister educating her three children in Botswana, where they are missionaries. It's not something we had ever thought of taking on ourselves. Up until this time we had both agreed that we couldn't home educate and were glad we could afford the Christian school. Even though between the ages of thirteen and fifteen I went downhill at school both academically and morally, I strongly resisted the idea that home education might be an acceptable option for our children. For me there were still too many things which I felt they would miss out on; I had not learned to think outside the box. At that time we had three boys; I thought they would miss things which only a school could offer, such as socialisation and sports – so I was opposed to the idea of taking them away from that. Both of us felt that the argument of school being a corrupting influence didn't really apply as the boys went to a school run by Christians, where the Word of God was taught and the teachers were morally upright people.

That year Andrea and the children had the opportunity to spend time in Botswana with her sister and brother-in-law. They were away for three months. The head teacher at the school was happy for the children to be away for such a long time as they were taking work with them and were effectively, going to be home educated. She knew we were praying about the possibility of home education and saw the visit, as we did, as an opportunity to spend the time waiting upon the Lord and seeing if it was possible to teach the children at home. We were still naturally resistant to the idea, but realised that the Lord was doing something in our lives. Andrea's sister was home educating her children as she didn't want to leave them behind in England at boarding school and sending them to a local school wasn't possible. We decided that we would review the situation when Andrea returned. She spent three wonderful months in Africa experiencing first-hand the joys of having her children with her throughout the day and being able to teach them *and* learn with them. She saw learning in a new context, and realised that education is not something which can be learned from a workbook, or fitted into a classroom.

By the time Andrea was due to come home she was convinced that the Lord wanted us to take the children out of school. Despite my original reservations, whilst they were away, I had also come to realise that home education *was* the right option. It was amazing that the Lord brought us both to this position at the same time, even though we were on different continents! When Andrea arrived back from Africa we told the head teacher that the boys wouldn't be returning to school. She was a godly woman and fully supported the decision we made. We didn't know what the future held and felt the weight of being responsible for our children's education, but we made the decision knowing it was the Lord's will and that He would guide us and strengthen us for the task. We began to research home education more by reading parent help books and joining the Home Service. The more we read, the more we realised how limiting a school education can be.

In the early days we continued with the ACE curriculum as it provided a safety net for us. It allowed Andrea to find her feet. We knew very few other home educating families and it was very much a case of one day at a time. As Andrea gained confidence she sampled other methods of learning so that today we do things very differently from when we first began. Our thinking now is that 'education is the lighting of a fire and not the filling of a bucket' and so we use a mixture of workbooks, reading together, outside exploration and interest-led learning, to light that fire in our children.

When we discussed how we would home educate, we knew it would require commitment on the part of us both. It was vital that I was very involved and not left on the periphery. Andrea would need hands-on support and my encouragement that she was doing a good job; the children would need to know that, although not there during the working day, I was as much involved in their education as Andrea was.

Our first six years of home educating took place in Manchester while I was working full-time in a city centre office. In many ways we were a typical city family with me being out of the home for ten hours each day. We had a routine but it was not really one with which we were happy and to a large extent I was absent from much of what the family were doing. Although I was one hundred per cent supportive of the choice we had made it was difficult to be practically involved. However, in 2003 we moved to Scotland and I began working from home. Although I still have a full-time job, because my office is in the home, I am much more involved in family life and am able to be more hands-on. All of life is a learning process and it is very precious to be so much more available to facilitate this process in the children. Our lives have changed for the better since our move and we have much more opportunity for outdoor experiences which are so valuable as a learning tool.

One book, amongst others, I have found helpful is *The Hands-on Dad* by Rick Boyer. In this book he outlines the responsibilities of home educating fathers (and indeed all fathers) and gives an outline of the sort of father that I really wanted to be. Amongst other things he encourages a father to be a provider, a motivator, a leader, a teacher and a disciplinarian. It takes a lot of thinking and re-thinking once you step onto the road of home educating your children and good parenting needs a constant re-evaluation of family life. My parenting has changed over the years, and I can honestly say that I don't think I would be half the father I have become (and I still have a long way to go!) if we had not stepped out onto that home education highway. I know that Andrea would say the same about herself as a mother. Home educating parents have to face issues straight on and have no one to delegate responsibility to. We believe that this is how it should be and taking full responsibility for the upbringing of our children is one of the positive aspects of becoming a home educating family.

The outline in *The Hands-on Dad* has helped enormously in being a guideline for my role in the following ways:

As *Provider* I am responsible for meeting the physical and material needs of my family, bringing home the money for food, clothing, shelter and relaxation. As a home educating father I am also ultimately responsible for providing the necessary resources to enable the children to learn at home. This includes workbooks, resources, field trips, and tutors if required. Ensuring that jobs around the house are done makes Andrea's 'job' of working with the children easier. Amongst other things I have rearranged shelves for educational resources, painted a wall to make a good background display and helped tidy up after a messy craft session. As we have five boys I am primarily responsible for providing the children with practical opportunities to learn; encouraging them to acquire different skills, assist with various jobs, and take up hobbies. In our home this includes woodwork, gardening and painting. We have tried to encourage the older boys to take part in various outdoor sports and activities that I can also be involved in like canoeing, mountain biking and camping. These provide invaluable bonding experiences and ideal opportunities for discussions on all manner of topics. There are times when others may have skills they can teach our children and I am responsible for ensuring that these people are of good character and will be an asset and not a liability to the children.

As a *Motivator* I can encourage and motivate, not only my children but also Andrea. Motivating others is not always an easy thing to do, especially at those times when I am finding it hard to motivate myself. But when Andrea feels weak spiritually, physically or mentally I have a responsibility to encourage her, however I am feeling. When she is having an 'off' day I should be there to tell her what a wonderful job she is doing! I endeavour to show interest in what the children are doing, encouraging and praising them as often as possible. It's easy to be critical of our children's efforts or to overlook what they are doing well. Praise when they have done their best can give them the impetus to keep trying when the going gets tough. Of course, this applies in all areas of their lives, from doing their academic work to building a godly character. Much of the time this can be given through words of encouragement but should also be as a result of my example to them.

As a *Leader* I am responsible for the major decisions which affect the family. Although leadership does not mean tyranny, there are times when someone has to make a final decision. Of course Andrea and I discuss everything as I value her wisdom greatly, but in the family situation as the head of the home, the ultimate responsibility is mine. If possible we try to make decisions as a family, with the older children having an input into those decisions that will affect them. It is not always easy to make decisions which will inevitably have an affect on so many people and I am aware that it is only by seeking God's will in prayer and through reading his word that the right decisions can be made. My other role as leader is to give my wholehearted support to each member, in their respective positions within the family and in the learning and/or career choices they make. My support for Andrea is critical as she carries on her day-to-day dealings with the children. Much of the choosing of educational experiences and resources is down to Andrea and she needs to know that I trust, respect and support her in this. If there are things that I feel are not suitable I have to be careful to give constructive criticism that will help rather than hinder her in any way.

Whilst I need to be a *Teacher* my role is different from Andrea's. My involvement in the day to day academics and formal learning experiences is far less. Our family tends to do most of the bookwork during the winter months. As soon as the sun comes out, we try to give the children the opportunity to be out and about experiencing 'real' education – hands-on learning through such activities as play, visits to museums and walks. As I am not always available to join in these activities because I am in full-time employment, albeit at home, my job is to teach in other ways. However even this is changing little-by-little. I have recently dropped two days each month from my office job and so can do more with the family on those days.

I have always taken the responsibility for teaching from Scripture at home; we commence every day with Bible reading, discussion, and prayer at the breakfast table. We also endeavour to have a family worship time after the evening meal once a week.

Of course I should also be teaching by example. I find this to be the hardest method of all but probably the most effective! I know how important it is to be prepared to patiently answer the children's questions and involve them in the things that I am doing so that they are learning alongside me. This might include taking at least one of them with me whenever I go into the forest to chop wood, taking them to the sawmill, or encouraging them to help me in the garden. These may all be jobs I could achieve far more quickly on my own, but they are wonderful learning opportunities for the children and well worth the time and effort it takes on my part.

I am also the principal *Disciplinarian*! This of course does not mean the sole disciplinarian. Working from home means

I am on hand to deal with serious discipline issues as and when they arise; being there to notice when the children need guidance on character traits that could become problematic if not dealt with promptly. This is one of the great advantages of home educating, seeing how our children behave throughout the day and not just at the beginning or end of it. As many parents will no doubt agree, administering discipline in the right way can be very difficult and requires wisdom and patience.

If I am to be the kind of father I should be and indeed want to be, I need to take an active role in the education of my children. I believe that the best way this can be achieved is by home educating them. I want to take the front seat and not a back seat when it comes to the way my children are raised. Parenting is a joint effort and having a full time job is not an opt-out clause, nor does it mean that the educating of children should all be down to the mother. I am accountable to God for the way my children are brought up. I am responsible for the way I talk to them, for the example I set them and for the encouragement (or indeed discouragement) I give them. Playing an active role in their education takes time, energy, wisdom and much prayer! Sometimes this means that sacrifices are necessary, but ultimately it is worth it as I know that I am building a solid foundation for the future of the children God has entrusted to me.

A person never regrets becoming a Christian and although the Christian life often isn't easy and we have problems and trials, there is always an underlying peace and contentment. This is also true of home education. We have never regretted the decision we made to have our children at home with us and to educate them ourselves. The further we go along this road the more sure we are that it is the right one, not only because of the state of the school system but because we actually believe that children learn more in an interest-led way. We know them better than anyone else and are best able to help them become the people God wants them to be; helping them to build on their strengths and interests and work on their weaknesses. We are the best people to talk to them about issues affecting their lives and the decisions they need to make. Because we know them so well we can help them sort out the confusion that can come from growing up in today's society. We love them more than anyone else does and want to see them set out into adulthood having thought outside the box; to help them to be comfortable with being different when to be different is right!

God has honoured the faltering steps we took when we began home educating our children all those years ago. Our desire to see them trained to become men and women of God is reaching fruition. We are still finding our feet and will be for a long time and, of course, our children are far from perfect. However, the older ones have given their lives to the Lord and want to go on for him. They are well-rounded, well-educated (whatever that means!), sociable, and are generally able to think things through for themselves. We know that God is blessing our weak attempt to be good parents and are not surprised when our children have the ability to do what we ourselves have encouraged them to do – to think outside the box.

Good Kite-flying Days

- Rachel Retallick
- Children – two boys and one girl
- Age range between eight and thirteen
- Living on Anglesey, North Wales
- Have always home educated

When I was seven my mother gave birth to my second brother. Sadly, complications with her labour meant that the baby, Paul, was severely brain damaged and given only a few days to live. Years later, when I had babies of my own, I realised the full significance of the phrase I often used when telling this story, 'We thought he would only live for a few days but in fact he lived for nine months'. Nine months! To a young mother, nine months is like a lifetime – it seems as if the baby has always been. My mother, who carried on as normal as far as I was concerned, spent much of each day while I was at school, travelling several miles to see Paul in hospital. She was able to help care for him, feeding him through a tube in his nose.

This may seem an odd way to begin an article about home education but the whole experience of Paul's life became foundational for mine. Through those many traumatic days we knew he might die at any time and I began to think seriously about life and death and what would happen to me if I died. My grandmother was staying with us and reminded

me that Jesus had died on the cross so that I could be for-
given and know that I would go to heaven to be with him.
We prayed together and I said I was sorry for my sins and
that I wanted to be a Christian and give my life to God.

Paul died in a beautiful way. He spent his last five weeks
at home and died in my mother's arms. I was in the bath
when my father told me, and my brother and I went downstairs and held him. We all cried together.

Life is very precious and incredibly fragile. Death is one of
life's inevitable events and yet so often we pretend it won't
happen to us. Knowing Paul taught me to live one day at a
time, to try to please the Lord at each stage of my life and not
to look to the future too much. It is good and right to plan
and prepare for times to come, but we do not know how
many days we have, so my aim has been to live each day
wisely. King Solomon wrote in Ecclesiastes 9:10, 'Whatever
your hand finds to do, do it with all your might, for in the
grave, where you are going, there is neither working nor
planning nor knowledge nor wisdom.' Because I educate my
children at home I am able to make the most of my time with
them and try to ensure that they are living in a way which
pleases God now.

In June 2005 my children and I went on holiday with my
father in his camper van. We explored an area of our beautiful island of Anglesey which we had not visited before. Near
Porth Eilian there is a lovely campsite which overlooks the
sea and lighthouse at Point Lynas. At a moment when the
children were at a loose end my father produced a small
pocket kite which he had brought, thinking it would provide
some fun sometime. We also had a larger kite given to us by
the campsite owner, one which someone else had lost earlier.
We had flown kites before and knew how best to get them in
the air but, try as we might, we couldn't get either to stay up.
One child would hold it in the air while the other started to
run with the string, all to no avail. The campsite had a rocky

outcrop in the centre which was excellent for running round. And run we did, mostly with the kites bouncing along the ground behind us. Occasionally they would stay up for a few seconds, but it was not very satisfying. It just wasn't windy enough.

A few weeks later we had planned a day on the beach with fellow home educators, the Hardy family from Manchester. The large kite came out again but on this blustery day, flying it was a completely different matter. The kite took off on its own and swooped high into the air. The only skill the flyer needed was to hold on tightly to the string!

One of the things I have discovered as a mother and home educator is that when the conditions are right, flying is easy! Watching the learning process of my babies and toddlers was one of the first things which led me to teach the children at home. They just grew – in all ways – so easily and naturally. I didn't want to interrupt this wonderful process by sending them away to school. I wanted to continue to be an intimate part of it; to be present all the time and therefore able to understand fully their developing gift of language; to guide them as they grew and to share the joy of a love of life and learning. So, much of my time was spent trying to ensure that the conditions for the children's growth, in every area of life, were as good as they could be. I described myself as a facilitator rather than a teacher.

One of the great joys of our home educating life has been our many trips and visits to places of interest. We started to explore our home area of Anglesey several years ago and still feel we are only scratching the surface. A visit to somewhere like the city of Bath is invaluable for its reinforcement of the history of the Georgian period, not to mention Roman and medieval history! And surely there is nothing quite so memorable as standing on HMS Victory (Nelson's flagship) or taking a boat trip round the present fleet at Portsmouth. Our life has been full of such delights, all recorded in diaries containing photos, leaflets and other souvenirs. Looking back over these ensures that nothing is forgotten and it consolidates the things learnt over the years.

Unfortunately, life is not always full of perfect kite-flying days. Sometimes things do not go to plan and everything seems very hard. In 2000, my husband, Simon, had a breakdown, following years of difficulties with work and periods of unemployment and struggling with the pressures of church and family. Later, he was diagnosed as having chronic fatigue syndrome. Sadly, problems in every area of his life made it impossible to live as a normal family and in April 2002 the children and I moved into rented accommodation two miles away. The stress and trauma of the years leading up to the move are indescribable. The breakdown of a marriage is tragic, but the children's relationship with their father has improved and is now much more stable.

So I became a single parent. Although lone parents are not stigmatised as they were in the past there is no doubt that becoming one is not a good career move! No longer could we be looked upon as an exemplary Christian family. However, there are always benefits to every situation and when you feel you are at the bottom of the heap it is good to know that you can't fall much further. Also, to be living in rented accommodation and facing the possibility of having to move if the landlord pleases, helps to remind you that nothing is permanent in life. I have found it easier to trust the Lord when times are hard and there are fewer external things on which to depend.

During the extremely difficult times of making life-changing decisions, moving house, sorting out finances, and endeavouring to provide for Simon's needs as far as possible, I tried to maintain a normal routine with the children, their education and outside activities. A few close friends and my father helped me keep my head above water, but without a doubt the continual, close and very evident presence of the Lord kept me going. For a very long time, whenever I felt down or needed some encouragement, the right word for the moment would be found in a daily text, personal Bible reading, or passage of Scripture (from *Keys for Kids*) shared with the children. God was faithful and carried me through. As time went by and I retold the story of our move, I was blessed by the response of my home educating friends who were, without exception, understanding and supportive. So many have helped me and upheld me in prayer and I feel very privileged to be part of such a wonderful community. The children and I have made many good and special friends through the Home Service's conferences as well as through events organised in the North West and Deeside Groups. Also the email forum, Deut 6v7, has been a tremendous encouragement. To know that at any one moment there are many others experiencing similar home educating joys and difficulties is a continuing source of help and, in times past, was almost literally a lifeline.

Having three children with you all the time is not easy but at the time of our move I was very grateful that they were close by and able to share in everything that happened. I felt sad when I remembered a story of a child who came home from school to a different house having played no part in his family's move. To include the children in as much of my life as possible has helped them, and me, to cope with its challenges. The many difficulties of life, worked through together, are another important means of growth. As Paul says in Romans 5:3–4, '. . .we also rejoice in our sufferings, because we know that suffering produces perseverance; perseverance, character; and character, hope.'

One of the wonderful things about home education has been the ability to study historical periods and base the rest of our work and reading around that time frame. It is exciting to see how art, literature, music and science all fit into their historical context. Much of the formal, more academic, work we have undertaken has been linked to our other activities, trips and interests of the moment. David and Hannah have tended to work together. Jonathan latches on to all he can and studies reading, English and maths at his own level. As the children get older we are working towards some exams but trying not to focus too much on them. We do not want to lose the freedom of home education by being too exam orientated but we find they are a good incentive to work hard and achieve more.

It is fascinating to watch the children's characters and natural leanings develop. Jonny is very good with his hands and delights in making things and doing woodwork with his grandfather. Hannah loves to play the piano in between writing, organising her Literary Society, cooking or planning special events. David reads avidly, enjoys sport and plays on the computer. The joy of home education is that we can follow our interests and catch up on other things quickly if we feel the need. Any weaknesses are addressed as and when necessary. This is the year for an extra emphasis on maths!

Since David was four I have recorded in detail the events of each day and everything each child has studied. Originally this was in case we were inspected by the Local Education Authority. However, I am also very interested in the learning process and so wanted to remember what we had done and when. I am so glad I have this record. When I feel we have not done much I can look back and see how hard we have worked – or not!

My biggest problem in life is getting up in the morning (having worked into the early hours)! However, once I have managed that, we have our breakfast and Bible reading together and start work. Because we often begin late (about 10.30 AM) we usually work until about 3.30 PM. As well as the work we do in the day, we enjoy many other so-called 'extra-curricular' activities. I actually view them as far more central to the curriculum – the curriculum of life!

Our week is shaped by our regular commitments. On Sundays we attend services at Ebenezer Evangelical Church in Bangor and in the afternoon have a walk and share fun and fellowship with some of our old friends from our previous church. They are like family to us and their knowledge and wisdom are a very enriching part of our lives.

On Mondays we all attend our local, highly respected, brass band, the Beaumaris Band. We have been fortunate to be able to borrow our instruments and to learn to play at the weekly rehearsals. After a stressful, busy day there is nothing like a good 'blow' to get things into perspective and lift the spirits. It is also nice not to be in charge and just to follow the conductor. David and I sit together and both do what we're told! Jonny joined the band this year and in the summer we all wore our red band tee-shirts and played together for the first time. It was a lovely feeling.

The children have all had swimming lessons. The exercise is beneficial, they have learnt to swim very well and love being in the water. I find it useful to have a few minutes of time to myself while watching them and have also enjoyed seeing someone else teach them. It was particularly interesting to see that the child who had difficulty concentrating at home also struggled on that front in the pool. Good to know it wasn't just me who was at fault!

Both in swimming and band the children are of mixed ages but grouped according to their ability. They are excellent 'home education friendly' activities! Adults are allowed to play in the junior band and I have found it humbling and helpful to learn with the children. It is good to be reminded of what it feels like to try very hard and still not always meet the mark!

On Tuesdays we have often gone to our local art group. It was set up by a friend of ours when Jonny was still a toddler and has given us many happy memories and a great delight in art. The aim of the group was to paint outside, which meant the children could draw or paint for as long as they could concentrate and then play. We've been to many beautiful locations and got to know lots of interesting people, also benefiting from the years of experience of local artists who have come to share their expertise with the group. We have visited exhibitions of their work and got to know their different styles. The Oriel at Llangefni, which is a wonderful friendly gallery and museum, is one of our favourite places, while the Ucheldre centre at Holyhead, which runs an annual Art for All exhibition, has enabled the children to exhibit the best of their year's art. It is a good incentive to keep producing work and to try hard.

On Wednesday and Friday evenings the children attend their respective youth activities at church.

We also have several annual events. In the summer we benefit from the United Beach Mission which runs activities on Benllech beach. The teams of varying ages entertain the children on the beach and teach them biblical truths. I took the children as soon as they were all old enough not to eat the sand! As little ones they loved the afternoon 'holiday specials' and now they support the team as much as possible and are looking forward to joining it when they are old enough.

In May we attend many of the concerts and talks organised by our local Arts Festival in Beaumaris. I took the children to talks when most people thought they were a bit too young to understand them, but because the talks were of an excellent standard the children were able to appreciate them at their own level and, as they have grown up, really look forward to this annual event. We can now go to more of the evening concerts too and delight in the high quality of the performances. I was thrilled this year to be approached by the wife of the Artistic Director who had seen us at many events over the years and wanted to know who we were. She approached me and said, 'I've seen you, and thought – home education?' I was really chuffed about that!

A summer camp with Mirfield and Dewsbury Evangelical Churches is a recent addition. David and Hannah attend as campers, Jonny as a junior camper, and I go and help with the cooking. We all have a good time, lots of outdoor activities and lovely evening meetings. I enjoy the freedom from the responsibility for the children and it is bliss to cook and not to have to wash the dishes!

Each year in November we hold a Tearfund coffee morning and evening in our house. We send out invitations, bake cakes and biscuits, clean and tidy the house (a job which is getting more difficult each year!) and our local representative comes and displays Tearfund products on every available surface. Last year we sold over £500 worth of goods. We also do a sponsored swim. It is good to remember those who are so much less well off than us and to feel that we are doing something, if only a little, to help.

I have now been home educating for nine years. I expected that by now I would be an expert on the subject, but instead I keep thinking of new questions which need answering. How can I maintain the joy and flexibility of our early years in the face of approaching exams? How and when do I find out what history (for example) Jonny has absorbed while working with David and Hannah? Will I be able to fill in the gaps in his knowledge effectively? But on a more down to earth level – when am I going to find time to clean the bathroom?

Walking by Faith, One Step at a Time

- Norman and Nicola Wells
- Children – five girls and one boy
- Age range between two and fourteen
- Live in West London
- Have always home educated

When our eldest daughter reached the age of four, neighbours and friends would say to her, 'You're a big girl now. You'll be starting school soon.' And she would look up at us, wide-eyed and ask, 'Am I, Mummy? Am I, Daddy?' And we would reply, 'Well, Mummy and Daddy haven't decided yet!'

When we had married eleven years previously, we had neither heard of home education nor met any home educating families. At that point, the education of any children we might have in the future seemed a far-off prospect to which we had given no thought at all. Nevertheless, during those early years of marriage the seeds of interest in a distinctively Christian education were sown within us and began to take root.

Several years before our first child was even a twinkle in her mother's eye, we attended a debate on education at a local church and found the case for an education based firmly on Christian principles far more convincing than the case against. Little-by-little we came to the view that if the Lord should bless us with children, we would want to provide them with a consistently Christian education, though what that would mean in practice was far from clear in our minds. If anyone had pressed us at that stage, we would probably have expressed the vague hope that there might be a Christian school within travelling distance if and when the time came.

The responsibility of parents

It wasn't until Nicola was expecting our first child that we began to come into contact with home educating families. We were very impressed with what we saw and were challenged to consider more carefully the biblical teaching on the responsibility of parents for all aspects of their children's upbringing. From Ephesians 6:4 we learned that fathers bear the chief responsibility for the education of their children in the broadest sense, and from Deuteronomy 6:4–9 we understood that parents are entrusted with the task of teaching their children the ways of God, both through times of formal instruction and informally in the context of everyday life.

In the book of Proverbs we saw example upon example of what it means to teach children 'when you sit in your house, when you walk by the way, when you lie down and when you rise up'. Large portions of the book are framed in terms of a father or mother's instruction of their children and it covers a staggering range of subjects. Taken as a whole, Proverbs showed us that wise parents will provide a broad, comprehensive and practical training in righteousness for their children, with a view to equipping them to lead a godly life in an ungodly world.

As time went on, we came to see that the basis for a consistently Christian education controlled and directed by parents does not rest on a few isolated passages of Scripture or even on a whole book of the Bible, but goes much deeper than that. After all, what are we here for? And what are our children here for? In the words of the Westminster Confession of Faith, 'The chief end of man is to glorify God and to enjoy him for ever.' We are not here by chance in order to enjoy ourselves, but we are here by design, to bring glory to our Creator and enjoy fellowship with him.

Guiding principles

We are still working through the implications of this for the education of our children, but as we do so we are guided by principles such as the following:

- Since the fear of the Lord is the beginning of knowledge (Proverbs 1:7), we teach children to seek God, fear him, study his Word and understand his truth and train them in godliness, diligence and servanthood.
- Since God is the One who has created all things and orders the universe, in science, maths and geography we teach his creative wisdom and give him the glory for his design.
- Since the Lord is King of all kings and governs the nations, we teach that he is the One who plans the course of history and works out his purposes in all that happens in this world.
- Since God is a God of beauty and holiness, in studying literature, music and art we seek to consider things which are pure and lovely (Philippians 4:8).
- We seek to encourage children to honour their parents, and grow in humility and service to others. We teach boys and girls to understand their distinctive God-given roles and to respect each other with purity and modesty.

Flexibility

But how has it all worked out in practice? That's not an easy question to answer because we have found that we constantly need to adapt. Teaching one child at the age of four while her eighteen-month-old sister takes her morning nap is obviously quite a different proposition from teaching five children aged five to fourteen, while their two-year-old sister is playing around them, having outgrown her need for a sleep in the middle of the day.

We have found that we need to be flexible and adapt to changing circumstances. Like many other families, we have long given up any attempt to replicate school in the home. So, while our older children do have a timetable to provide some kind of structure and to encourage a disciplined approach to their studies, they are not required to stick to it rigidly.

At the moment, our oldest two (aged fourteen and eleven) work mainly by themselves on maths and English, allowing Nicola to spend time working with the next three (aged nine, seven and five). We do a fair amount as a family, reading together and working on projects. Our two-year-old potters around, joins in a bit and plays by herself quite happily most of the time. The older children are also willing and able to spend time with the younger ones.

We have never followed a set curriculum, but have tended to create our own from a variety of sources, often using material that others have passed on to us or that we have borrowed from the home schoolers' library in London. Our older children have used Saxon maths and A Beka science books, and we have used *Our Island Story* as a basis for teaching the history of Britain, supplementing it with other material and visits.

Benefits

Some time ago we asked our two oldest children, then aged eight and five, what they liked about being home educated and were heartened by their positive and enthusiastic response. This is what they said:

1. 'You can get more help at home than at school'

At home we can give our children far more individual attention than would be possible in a class of thirty. As parents, we know the characters of our children, we know their interests, we know how they learn and we know what they are capable of. All this puts us in a strong position to teach them a new concept or help them when they are struggling.

2. 'At school, you might be going over what you've already learned'

In the home you can tailor the instruction to the needs and ability of each child and let them go at their own pace. For example, some of our children have picked up new mathematical concepts very quickly and have been able to move swiftly on to the next lesson, without being frustrated by our insistence that they do exercise after exercise. Some have struggled and needed to proceed at a slower pace. With them, we can take more time and give them more practice or, where necessary, leave the topic for a while, returning to it at a later date. Often after a break of a few weeks or months, whatever it was they were agonizing over clicks into place straight away.

3. 'You don't have to do schoolwork all day'

In the home it is possible to use time far more efficiently than in the classroom. As a general rule, we concentrate on more formal book-based learning in the mornings, leaving the afternoons free for shopping, cooking, crafts, music practice, gardening, playing games and spending time with friends. As our children grow older, we would like them to be available to help in the church and the wider community. There will always be the sick and elderly who will value their company and practical help. And learning to serve others is an important but often overlooked aspect in a child's education.

4. 'You can spend more time at the park and the library'

Such visits don't have to be hurriedly crammed in between being picked up from school and getting home in time to prepare the evening meal. When we look back to our own school days we recall getting home at about 4.30 PM absolutely exhausted and crashing out in front of the television until dinner time. Then, after dinner, we would often be up in our bedrooms from 7–10 PM doing our homework or revising for exams. We have made it a priority to try to ensure that our children are able to spend plenty of unhurried time with the rest of the family.

5. 'You're with Mummy all day . . . and you can play more with your baby sister'

With five daughters and one son, there has often been a baby sister to play with, but whether there is a baby in the home or not, one of the things that has always impressed us about home educating families is the love and respect the children show to their parents, and their willingness to help care for younger brothers and sisters.

6. 'When you're at home, your mum and dad know what you are doing'

If we are serious about training our children in godly ways, that is so important. We have been able to exercise a much closer control over the influences our children are subject to. They have been spared much of the peer pressure which contributes to the downfall of so many, and we have been able to speak to them about sinful attitudes and behaviour as they arise.

7. 'You have more friends'

Perhaps of all our daughters' comments this is the one that is the most hotly disputed. While children in school will generally be acquainted with a larger number of children their own age than those taught at home, the deepest and most lasting friendships are often forged not in the playground, but in the home.

In common with many other home educated children, our own children are amused whenever they hear 'socialisation' raised as an objection to home education. They are mixing with other people – of all ages – all the time, whether it be neighbours, shopkeepers, friends at church, other families at our monthly home schoolers' group, or visitors to our home. In addition to welcoming friends into our home for Sunday lunch most weeks, whenever we go away on holiday we try to meet up with some other home educating families and thus further extend our circle of friends. Our older children correspond on a regular basis with several close friends and one of the highlights of recent years has been a week away with fifty or so other home educating families.

8. 'You've got more time to read Bible stories' and 'You can learn more about God'

Whatever else our children study and whatever else they learn, we have sought to make the teaching of the Bible a priority in our home. It is, after all, the Word of God that is able to make them 'wise unto salvation'; it is those who meditate on the Word of God day and night who will flourish spiritually and it is those who have stored the Word of God in their hearts who are equipped to avoid sin.

We have used a number of means to try to ensure that the Scriptures are central to our family life.

(a) Family worship   At the beginning of each day after breakfast, and towards the end of each day after our evening meal, we gather together for a Bible reading and prayer. Our normal pattern is to read a passage of Scripture; briefly comment on it and apply it, asking the children questions as

we do so, and then to lead in prayer. When I am present I lead our family worship times, with Nicola taking the lead in my absence.

Over the years we have also used a number of books to help us explain and illustrate the teaching of the Bible. We often sing together – sometimes a verse or two of Scripture, occasionally a hymn or song, but more frequently, a Psalm.

(b) Personal Bible reading   When our children learn to read, we give them their own Bible and encourage them to read a short portion each day by themselves. We also encourage them to keep a small notebook where they can jot down anything that has particularly struck them, or make a note of any questions that have occurred to them so that they can ask later.

(c) Bible memorisation   In addition to learning isolated verses of Scripture together, we have found it helpful to memorise some longer passages of Scripture as a family. Often when we are learning a portion of Scripture, we write it out and put it up on the back of the bathroom door or in the children's bedroom, as a constant reminder to them.

(d) Preaching   Each Sunday morning and evening, we attend a church where we can hear the Bible expounded and applied. Our older children also join us at the church midweek Bible Study and Prayer Meeting.

Service

Sometimes people say to Nicola, 'I don't know how you do it – looking after those six children, and doing all the washing, all the cooking, all the cleaning – and teaching them at home as well!' But Nicola would be the first to admit that she doesn't do it all by herself! She has at least four assistants – including two very accomplished helpers, who are well able to assist her with the household chores.

On the fridge, just inside our back door, we've got a job chart for the week, showing who is responsible for what. We see it as a vital part of our children's education to teach them to function as members of a family; to cultivate in them a servant heart; to encourage them to look out for ways of helping and serving others and to do it cheerfully, without bitterness or resentment. Such things do not come naturally and the lessons are not always learned as swiftly as we would like, but they are well worth teaching. The more time we spend together, talking to each other, working and serving together, the more our family life is enriched.

Enriching family life

One other way in which we have found that home education has enriched our life together as a family is by doing some project work together. Over the years we have undertaken several projects where all the children have been able to contribute or take part in some way.

For example, during the course of a project on sheep farming and wool, we learned which countries produced wool and where different breeds of sheep were reared (geography); we learned about the weight of the fleeces before and after they were washed, the time it takes to shear one sheep and how long it takes to shear a flock of 125 sheep (maths); and we visited an old woollen mill while we were on holiday (history), and made some felt from scratch. We studied the processing of wool and obtained samples at different stages in the process from the Wool Marketing Board (technology); we conducted experiments into the properties of wool, comparing it with other materials (science); and we learned what the Bible has to say about sheep and shepherds (Bible study).

We have also studied several countries together. While learning about China, Nicola read some library books to the children and then they drew maps of the physical landscape, showing where various industries were located. They read about Gladys Aylward; plotted her journey on the map and also learned about the communist revolution in China. We then visited some friends who had lived in China. After sharing a Chinese meal with them, they taught us some Chinese words and Chinese songs and showed us some calligraphy and other things they had brought back with them. We also tried some Chinese painting. It would have been nice to finish off the project with a trip to China, but we did the next best thing and spent an afternoon in Chinatown in London!

Coping in the hard times

Lest anyone should be thinking that we have presented an unrealistically rosy view of our family's experience of home education, let us hasten to add that we have had our share of difficulties and trials. In addition to the inevitable periods of illness, it has been a struggle to continue with our normal schedule during early and late pregnancy and during the initial weeks following the birth of a child. During the past seven years, we have also suffered the loss of four children, three through early miscarriages and one at full-term. Yet even during these times of sadness, we have never regretted our decision to home educate, and during our times of loss we have taken great comfort from being surrounded by our children. After our son, Nathaniel, died inexplicably just a matter of hours before his birth, our other children appreciated being at home together. It was unthinkable to them that if they had been in school they would have been expected to carry on as usual.

Do we believe our children's education suffers as a result of these difficult times? Not at all! Even though the time-tables may go out of the window for a while and only a limited amount of bookwork is done, our children are learning lessons for life; they are receiving an education in and for the real world.

During times of difficulty, whether they are related to sickness, bereavement, squabbling children, being worn down by criticism, or whatever, we have found three things have helped us:

(1) Taking a long-term view of things

There have been periods when we have felt we are not achieving anything. But when we have looked back over a longer period – perhaps over six months or a year – things can look quite different. For this reason we have found it valuable to keep a brief daily record of the work we have done with our children, and the work and reading they do by themselves. Nicola keeps a notebook for this purpose and then writes up what each child has done every year. Some years we think to ourselves, 'I'm sure we haven't covered as much ground this year as last year', but when it's all written down, we begin to realise just how much progress the children have made.

(2) Fellowship with others of like-mind

We have found great value in meeting up with other home educators in formal or informal settings to share ideas and bear one another's burdens. In addition to our regular monthly get-together for Christian home educating families in our area, we always try to get along to any parents' evenings or conferences and when we're away on holiday try to meet up with other families. The Deut6v7 email list has also been a great help in overcoming any feelings of isolation.

(3) Remembering first principles

When the going gets tough, we remind ourselves why we are teaching our children at home. God has convicted us that it is our responsibility before him to bring them up in his ways; we are seeking to give them a Christ-centred education, an education rooted in the fear of God. Biblical truth is intensely practical. In the midst of trials of any kind, we come back to basics: God is in control; he sees; he knows; he cares; he is working out his purposes; he will give us all the grace we need. He will honour those who honour him – and he 'is able to do exceeding abundantly above all that we ask or think, according to the power that works in us' (Ephesians 3:20 NKJV).

Pressing on . . .

It hardly seems possible that more than a decade has passed since our eldest daughter confidently asserted that 'Mummy and Daddy hadn't decided' whether or not she would attend school. Looking back, we think Mummy and Daddy had pretty much decided, but telling other people that we were planning to home educate seemed such a huge obstacle. (It's not just children who have peer pressure to contend with!) But having crossed that bridge we've never looked back. The Lord has provided for us in so many ways. He has given us friends, help, encouragement, and sometimes even curriculum materials that have been passed on.

As we have gone on, things that at one time looked like mountains now look like mere molehills. Now, with our eldest daughter coming up to fifteen, there are other issues appearing on the horizon: exams – to do or not to do? And if 'to do', which ones? Then there is future employment and of course, in time, the whole question of courtship and marriage. But we go on, looking to the Lord, trusting him,

praying for wisdom and searching the Scriptures for light
and understanding on all these things. That is what the life
of faith is all about and God has given us some wonderful
promises to give us confidence along the way.

> If any of you lacks wisdom, let him ask of God, who gives to all
> liberally and without reproach, and it will be given to him.
> (James 1:5 NKJV)

From Negative to Positive

- Mike and Jan Matthews
- Children – two girls and two boys
- Age range between twenty-seven and thirty-five
- Mike and Jan now live in Pembrokeshire
- Home educated for sixteen years

Why did two relatively sane people like Mike and Jan home educate?

We had four children, two girls in quick succession then a gap of five years before having two boys in quick succession. We began home education in 1976 and finished in 1993. All our children have gone to sixth form college and university, thankfully without having sustained too many horrific effects educationally whilst in our hands! They are all Christians, happily married to Christians, and we praise the Lord for all his goodness to us. Our children have aged us into grandparents with four grandchildren.

Although some may think I'm well past it, being a pensioner with a free bus pass, being older does have some advantages, albeit few! A major advantage is the ability to take a step back and see how the whole educational spectrum has gradually evolved over the years, with all the changes in trends and shifts in attitudes, which continue to bewilder everyone.

Education has always been a political football, with the current ideas often at variance with the experience of teachers generally and at odds with lessons learnt from the past. The purposes and aims of education have always appeared to be somewhat hazy and this has been particularly true in regard to the Christian faith. Christian standards are continually being eroded and a syncretistic mix and match attitude to religion has crept in. There is the attitude that everyone makes their own belief system and each one is valid, as long as it is seen as being politically correct. Where an enfeebled and distorted version of Christianity is presented, this often acts as an inoculation against the Christian faith. I would emphatically say that were we in the position of new parents today, the reasons to home educate would be even more valid, with so many hot issues coming into very sharp focus. Home education is a precious liberty which is now under threat, and fellow Christians are unlikely to come to our aid once this freedom is seriously questioned because they are largely uninterested and do not see the need. I would encourage Christian parents to be proactive now while the liberty to do so remains.

Was the decision to home educate a sudden flash of inspiration? Well, not really but it was rather like hopping along a series of stepping stones, and I will begin at the first one.

I taught in primary schools for six and a half years before having my first baby. Like most other teachers, I had grown up in the state educational system and loved my job but whilst working as a teacher, some concerns uncomfortably forced their way into my thinking. They say that you don't really know a man until you are married to him; in just the same way you don't know the school staff until you have worked alongside them for some considerable time. This led to my first major concern. Teachers are a normal cross-section taken from society at large, exhibiting varied personal, beliefs, values and mindsets. They are not some alien species that children, and sometimes parents too, imagine them to be. Some teachers were really charming, others less so and a few were not nice people in any sense at all. Most teachers were as you might expect, worldly with non-Christian lifestyles. I could see that worldly teachers, even if their teaching skills were good, with their pupils achieving the highest possible grades, might still instill values and attitudes which I would consider negative. Codes of conduct and character shaping are even more vital than training the mind and any teacher who was an unbeliever was bound to have spiritually defective attitudes. If Christians are far from perfect in this realm, how much more is the person who is not influenced by the Scriptures? I would want a teacher to be someone able to see and correct character faults, who would not actively encourage further faults such as pride; I would want to see that teacher encourage positive traits in the children. Sadly many Christians are well aware of the danger of wrong teaching but are not conscious of the implications of wrong character training or of the social issues involved.

I was well aware that as a teacher I had the children's best waking hours and the parents had the time when the children were tired and least receptive. The children accepted what I said at face value and their trust in me was all too apparent. This raised my second concern; the content of the education with the child's predisposition to accept what was being taught. Children can be so easily manipulated. My concern was not just focused on the obvious topics of evolution or even wrong sexual counselling which can be corrected by a concerned parent to some extent. It was those lessons which were shaped or influenced by such wrong beliefs and which run right through secular education, which are far harder to correct. A person's angle in teaching literature or history for instance, may be coloured by such beliefs and that is far more subtle.

Thirdly, some material presented was just plain sinful and would pollute a child's mind: even at that time some sex education material was pornographic, but the most disturbing material was not so obvious. Some teachers with different standards were happy with things I found offensive.

My fourth worry was the content of a child's day which was unsupervised, whether it be in the playground, outside the school gates, or just the books available in the school library. Many books were clearly unacceptable from a Christian point of view though some might have been useful if there had been the right input by a responsible adult.

For all these reasons, I was now convinced there was a good case for Christian education. When my daughter went to infant school for two terms, these reasons became more apparent when viewed from the other side of the classroom door. We had little control over what went on in the classroom and our opinions were not sought or wanted. She went to a typical infant school and I would question her faithfully every day about what she had learnt and done. Gradually over the ensuing years I was taken aback at how much wrong thinking she had imbibed from those two terms, which I had not grasped at the time, including teaching about witches and magic. As a teacher I was unaware of much that was being taught in other classes and so it was not really surprising I was so ignorant of what went on in my daughter's class. My daughter then started to come home with scratches on her face but her teacher had said she should fight back. This meant that the friendliness between my daughter and her younger sister disappeared, to be replaced by a much more aggressive attitude. This emphasised the fact that her teacher was virtually a stranger to me, yet I was entrusting my precious daughter to her care. I also found my daughter was very bored for much of the time because the education did not seem to be tailored to individual children.

As parents, we began talking about home teaching but in a rather 'of course we wouldn't do it, would we?' sort of way.

However the Lord had other ideas and some unforeseen circumstances pushed us into it. Initially we believed a Christian school would be ideal, but as no Christian school was available, thought home education was the next best thing. We were surprised to learn home education can in fact be better. Obviously we would want as many options open to parents as possible and, as every family has different circumstances, each must choose what suits them.

At this stage our reasons were still mainly negative rather than positive but when faced with the immediate prospect, we gave it real thought and became enthused as we saw the possibilities opening up. Our reasons for home education rapidly became wholly positive. My major handicap was that it was more difficult for an ex-classroom teacher to start from scratch and evaluate the whole meaning of education. I suddenly had to rethink everything because I now had a totally different scenario. I was to discover that working alongside children, learning together in such small numbers was so liberating. Gone for ever was the chalk and talk mentality. I had to rethink what to teach and why it should be taught, then how and when to teach it. Methods and aims were called into question. What was our overriding purpose? For the first time, I had to think biblically about God's purposes in training children.

If I was going to teach from a Christian perspective, I would have to look at the whole world as belonging to the Lord, and that included geography, history, English and everything else. Suddenly subjects were exciting because they had a focus and an association, besides having this far deeper meaning. We could present a Christian worldview, an integrated Christ-centred view, where we were investigating God's world of science and mathematics, where we could see how the Lord was at work among the nations in times past and in the present day. We could appreciate how the Lord had gifted people in music, art, literature and languages. Education was becoming integrated in purpose and content, so far removed from the sterile adherence to chance and uncertainty, where the individual matters so little. Our children could see themselves in relation to God's world and were learning to think for themselves from a biblical perspective. It is thrilling to watch such a perception grow in a child, knowing that a sure foundation is being laid.

Education is a preparation, but a preparation for what? Once we saw our aim was to train the children to live obediently before the Lord, seeing things from a Christian standpoint, equipping them to be productive in his service so that they would become useful and good citizens, then that enlarged our horizons to an awesome degree. The scope was indeed vast and glorious. My task included the training of my children's characters according to the standards set out in God's Word, whilst not smothering but developing their personalities. Surely this was a precious work to be undertaken with a prayerful concern for their souls. We did not enjoy an entirely peaceful and quiet life, for if we embark on any spiritual battle, there will be a struggle. There would be days when Mum was tetchy and the children were squabbling, but because we relied on the Lord's strength rather than on our own, he was gracious and gave us the willpower to stay the course. We were all too well aware as parents that we had to live out what we were teaching. This meant we had to be consistent in reinforcing good attitudes and correcting bad ones, which was not always easy when we were tired or inclined to be selfish. Again the Lord honoured us because we were trying, however inadequately, to honour him. We needed to show self-control and had to teach our children to be self-controlled in all their behaviour, including how to control their viewing of television or listening to music.

We quickly came to realise education was not an isolated activity but part and parcel of normal waking life, just as described in Deuteronomy 6:7. We could be busy learning about the real everyday world in practical situations – such as taking care of siblings or preparing lunch, home decorating or gardening. As a family we had scope for meeting and being helpful to others. Without the dreaded peer pressure and problems due to a generation gap, we could be united and learn how to stand apart and be different in a world which longs to conform you to its image. It meant we were bonded closer as a family, for our children were not living in a different world with its separate language and culture. Family life was easier. We surprised many people by saying how much we enjoyed our teenage children's company and we truly meant it.

It was a real delight that our children's education could be tailored to their individual needs, interests and aptitudes. It could be such fun discovering their different talents and abilities. As parents we could also learn from the children and before long they overtook us in many areas. They had the disconcerting habit of proving they had better memories! We could all learn from visiting guests and this taught our children that we had something to learn from everyone, whether from hearing about their past experiences or from the God-given gifts they manifested. Sometimes we were delighted with our own progress in some hitherto misunderstood area in our own education and our children could see learning was an ongoing process for us. They could go at their own pace, although sometimes they had to go at ours, which might be slower! We suddenly had all the flexibility we could wish for in deciding our curriculum, daily schedules and holidays.

Do I have any reservations about home education? I am convinced that many worries people have are not actually real problems. These worries include no teaching experience and a lack of skills in certain specialist areas. Home education is all about learning together, mums and dads, children, tiny tots and grandparents, perhaps even the family dog! Once children are taught how to learn, then they will happily go on learning throughout their lives. We shouldn't be intimidated about the brilliance of others but stay focused on our own aims. The Lord will equip as necessary. My real reservations are that disunity on this subject between husband and wife will make home education very difficult, and if parents are unable to communicate easily with their children this too will be a serious drawback. Obviously there is a need to be temperamentally suited to working with children most of the time and other factors such as health and individual circumstances may have to be taken into consideration. Otherwise my advice would be 'go for it', enjoy, and have fun, all in the Lord's strength. Hopefully some day like us, you too will go on to share in the delight of exploring God's world with your own grandchildren.

Finding Our Rhythm

- Mark and Kate Charlesworth
- Children – four boys
- Age range between seven and fourteen
- Living in East Somerset
- Have home educated for six years

Welcome to our home schooling story which, I think, begins even before we had children. Mark and I would dream of how we would both work part-time and share the care of our children. This in reality didn't work out; not for the next nine years and a lot of life experiences later anyway! I think deep down we always held on to this vision and God has restored it to us. Now we both share our time between home and work which gives us and the children a broader experience. We have always wanted to limit the world's influence on our children, and to give them a good foundation in knowledge and understanding of the Christian faith, but knew nothing of the possibility of *not* sending them to school.

As we took Jacob (our eldest son) to school during his first few weeks and months, I remember feeling a growing unease about handing him over to someone who we knew nothing about, for seven of the best hours of his day, five days a week. The teacher wasn't a Christian so didn't share our strong faith in Christ. We knew nothing of her moral, ethical and social standards and how these permeated her teaching methods and preferences. When she had a nervous breakdown and left during the spring term of his first year we decided to take him out of school, feeling at least he would be happy at home.

I attended a couple of Education Otherwise meetings with him only to find that many of the people there appeared to hate the system. They also all seemed to have exceptional children, so I felt intimidated and put off by what struck me as a very negative attitude towards the school system. After all, I was a product of it and ninety nine per cent of our friends sent their children there; it had to be viewed differently for me. I felt very unsupported at the time and didn't know where to seek help in our desire to look at the possibility of home schooling Jacob.

So we found a local school and he went there and plodded on. He was never really happy and in the two schools he attended he was bullied and learnt to play the clown to cover up his insecurity and growing feelings of inadequacy. This eventually became more serious and turned into stomach pains each morning before going to school.

By this time Daniel had started school. He loved it and thrived, although when he was seven he did wander off from class to watch the dinner ladies set lunch as it was more interesting than drawing around his feet in the class. The teacher was most upset and asked me to have a serious talk with him. Well, I was torn because my heart was saying; 'Good on you for showing initiative to wander off and find something more interesting to do and *not* becoming disruptive,' but my mouth had to say, 'You have to conform, no matter what you think.'

We felt our children were suffering from being squeezed into the world's mould. And being taught by an atheistic system, their characters didn't seem to have the freedom to develop. I had a picture in my mind of our four boys leaving home and walking out through our gate; what did I want for them at that time? I wanted them to have a sound knowledge and experience of our faith, a strong sense of security in their own masculinity and to be able to communicate well and relate well to women. We had to ask ourselves if the state system would provide that. After six months of prayer and discussion we took them out of school. Our boys were then aged nine, seven, five and two-and-a-half.

We'd faced the 'jumping-off-a-cliff' feeling about taking them out of school only to find that when we did so, it wasn't daunting at all.

I started by buying a few books from WH Smith and saying to the boys if they wanted to do some bookwork they could, but they didn't have to. I told Jacob, who had struggled and resisted reading, that I'd never *make* him read. Within a few weeks he wanted to read the cereal packets at breakfast and slowly he began the long process of becoming the confident, competent reader which he now is at thirteen!

We took months to discover what would work for us as far as structure goes. Finally now we have a pattern. During the first year it was trial and error and at times we felt as if we'd swapped one set of stress you could blame on someone else for another that was all our responsibility! But through that we began to see Jacob uncoil and relax and to start to enjoy life. We have a 'structure with flexibility' pattern so have used curricula that don't require lots of box ticking (too much pressure and stress!) We used *Learning Adventures*, which is a topic-based curriculum covering from Ancient Egypt to the Age of Exploration. For this you need a Bible, some of the recommended historical fiction and the folder. It takes you on a journey and you become immersed in the topic for a term, or half a term, covering every subject except maths.

We have tried to branch off for the boys to do their own projects but it hasn't really worked. They prefer a little structure to work within. We've enjoyed topic-based banquets and meals and invited our extended family to come and see their work as I feel that it's good for them to have it seen and appreciated by others and it encourages them to take pride in the presentation. Having informed the Local Education Authority of our intention to home educate, we have a visit every eight to twelve months. The lady who has come recently just praises all that they do and has loved seeing any displays we may have up.

We keep roughly to school term times, (unless we want to get something finished) because the boys want to see friends who have been in school and because we need a break! We often find that 'out of school time' is when a lot gets explored – we have had some of our most successful, in depth discussions at teatime! Our conversations can often be rich and rewarding and we've found that the children's inquisitiveness is heightened by being at home and being unafraid to ask.

When I took Jacob out of school, I felt that he wouldn't have enough exposure to the variety of art experiences that I wanted, especially as he loves artwork and drawing. For this reason I set up a fortnightly art group for local home schoolers which has been really successful over the last four and a half years. We have drawn on a lot of local talent, asking people to come and teach a group of up to twenty children aged six to fourteen(!) and they *love* our children. We've made a patchwork banner and put it up in the local library as a display of our work. Sometimes I think that the actual art has been secondary to the boys enjoying being with their friends, doing something creative.

We've always encouraged the boys to go to local clubs and so now we have them involved in a variety of social settings from gym club to badminton and Beavers to Scouts.

Sometimes I still have days when I *do* 'school at home' and I feel frustrated when the children haven't 'done enough'.

I think this stems from my schooled view of learning. Those days never leave me with a feeling of satisfaction or as if I've followed the Lord's leading.

We have other days when I'm relaxed, have taken time to still myself before God for a few minutes and the children are relaxed. We finish bookwork by eleven o'clock and they are off doing lots of exciting play. Sometimes we end up talking about far-ranging subjects and they are eager to listen. This sounds idyllic but it does happen sometimes I promise! I have learnt so much, not just in the vast range of things we've learnt together, but in un-learning my pre-conceived ideas about how children learn and what they need to learn.

During the early days I read a really inspirational American book called *A Patchwork of Days* by Nancy Lande, in this book people wrote about a day in their home school life. I learnt that every family has its own rhythm to find. This helped when we found that although a neighbour of ours also home schools, we have very little to do with each other in terms of the bookwork or project side of things, although we occasionally share resources. We do however find that both adults and children enjoy friendship, empathy and a common vision.

It's all about perspective and having a relaxed outlook that if it doesn't work by ten o' clock we ditch the books and go out for a walk with the dog. When we come back we have a tea break and a biscuit and I read a book to them. These days I'm finding it's not what they learn that's important, because they seem to forget a fair bit of it; but *how* they learn to learn so that they don't forget.

After the 'socialisation question' the thing everyone asks is, 'What about exams?' Well, at the moment we're just making the most of our precious time with our even more precious children, watching them grow and 'grow up' in the best environment that we know. We have to believe that

God gave these wonderful people to us for our wise stewardship and if we have the strength of conviction to believe him, and not the world, he will bless our family in the decisions we make for the future and bless our community through us.

Christian Education, a Whole Life Experience

- Randall and Mary Hardy
- Children – four boys and two girls
- Age range between ten and twenty-seven
- Living in Manchester
- Have home educated for sixteen years

Looking back

We must be getting old or at least looking old these days, because people keep asking us retrospective questions about home education such as, 'If you could have your time over again, would you do the same thing?'

'Yes, most certainly,' we reply. Maybe we would do things slightly differently next time, but we have absolutely no regrets about our involvement with Christian education for over twenty years. In fact we are really grateful to God for awakening us at the time he did to the various choices we could make educationally. Right now our six children range in age from twenty-seven to ten, and it was when the eldest was three or four that we became aware of Christian education. To cut a long story short, our oldest three spent their school years at Covenant Christian School in Stockport, while we as parents received as much education during that time as they did.

Prior to that it felt as if most of our Bible knowledge was

on one side of a coin and all our other knowledge and information about the world around us was on the other side; there was very little meshing of the two. Being exposed to a situation where there was a real attempt to find out what God has to say about any topic being taught was such a good experience. We were encouraged to look through Christian glasses at the world around us and to try and communicate to the children that they lived in a world whose Maker and Sustainer is God, which gives him control over history, the affairs of men, the future, and indeed everything. This was no superficial veneer of Christianity on top of a secular education – it was different from the inside out.

As the years went on, we knew it was God's will that we should move into teaching the younger three at home, but we have still adhered to many of the same principles. In fact, it seems to us now that the most important issue is whether or not a child is receiving a thoroughly Christian education. Whether that is delivered in a home setting or a Christian school is ultimately of less significance, although we lean towards the home/family environment as the first option to be seriously considered.

From time to time we come across people who have taken children out of school because the 'one size fits all' education which was on offer did not suit their child for whatever reason. Those children will surely do better and feel more positive when their particular needs are understood and met by a committed adult in an almost one to one ratio. But home education per se is no guarantee of Christian content; we really have to look to the Lord to provide us with, or inspire us to create, cohesive Christian content in our plan of work if we want to make a lasting difference to our children's lives.

With all our mind

Jesus said that the greatest commandment is to love the Lord our God with all our heart, soul, mind and strength. It gradually dawned on us that having received a secular education ourselves, loving God with all of our mind involved a serious process of change. Yes, we sat in school assemblies before multi-faith approaches came along; yes, we got good reports from the Scripture teacher and even learned one or two Bible passages off by heart. But we never connected these with the rest of life in such a way as to develop a Christian mindset, so Romans 12:2 was a real challenge to us in our early adult years as young believers. It tells us not to be conformed to this world, but to be transformed by the renewing of our minds, that we may prove what the will of God is. We have had to unlearn the mindset of having Scripture in a separate compartment from all other knowledge, and learn how to teach from a God-centred starting place.

Worldviews – what are they?

What we discovered is that the real difference between educational approaches is to be found not in style of delivery or methodology but in the underlying worldviews or philosophies of life. Many people think education is about passing on facts and skills to others so that they can be equipped to live. However, that is only the shopfront, and behind it lie the deeper issues, our understanding of life and how the world works. Like most parents of young children, we didn't understand back then that one of the perils of exposure to secular schooling is the fact that worldview is one of those things which is 'caught' as well as 'taught'. Teachers inevitably communicate their own values and attitudes for better or for worse and children under their tutelage will absorb them.

With many years of our own re-education behind us, we now appreciate what our primary concerns for our children should be. First of all to know what worldviews they are being exposed to and secondly, what values they are absorbing. This is important so that in time they will be able to refine their own worldview in the best way possible. Even Christian curricula need assessing for their ability to foster a Biblical worldview, for unless they do, they are not truly Christian. This is much needed, for too many adult Christians continue for years after their conversion with a non-Christian worldview. Now, with the hindsight of over twenty years' experience of Christian education, we are more convinced than ever that our first calling as parents is to impart a worldview to our children which has the Lord as the beginning and the end in all things. Equipped with this foundation they will have good ground in their hearts to build with him in the future wherever he leads them.

We began to investigate Christian education as a result of the Lord prompting us to do so. At that stage we had a basic but rather uninformed desire to put our children on a good foundation to know the Lord and be good all-rounders, coping well with life in this world. It was only later we came to realise that whatever our own worldview was, our children were going to assimilate it. Therefore we had a lot of catching up to do! We doubt if any of us has escaped totally from the worldview we ourselves were fed as children, and the residue is one of the things we should be inviting the Holy Spirit to refine out of us. Hence we have only been a step or two in front of our offspring for much of the journey! First we had to grasp the scope of the Bible for ourselves, see its application to issues, then communicate it in a relevant way – and the process is ongoing.

What is ordinary?

Over the years we have come to realise that in Britain, ordinary education is secular. And a secular understanding of life considers the Lord irrelevant to everything except the residue of religious superstitions that some people fail to shake off. This is most obvious in the science of origins, but it pervades the whole of the curriculum, right through to the things we perceive as neutral. Christian education places the Father, the Son and the Holy Spirit as central to everything past, present and future. There is no area where God is not relevant. We came to realise that if Christian parents do nothing in the area of educational choice, the default position will be to impart a secular education, just because ordinary education here is secular, and the ways we all think and behave have been absorbed from our forebears by something resembling osmosis (1 Peter 1:18). If, as parents, we want something different for our children it will require a definite decision, plus courage and perseverance to implement it.

Long-term work – beware discouragement!

One area where we easily fell prey to discouragement was over the matter of not seeing the finished work for so long. It is so easy to lose heart or to fail to be content because the work is still in progress, rather than being thankful for small stages completed along the way. We needed to believe that if we sow to the Spirit, we will (in due time) from the Spirit reap eternal life. Another aspect we forgot was that building sites are always messy places whilst work is going on – sometimes we condemn ourselves because things are not just as we would like them to be, or drive ourselves with unrealistic agendas. The important thing is that the project continues under the Lord's direction until the end – as children reach adulthood, they will assume responsibility for themselves, and we will have less input. Until then, we are to be obedient servants, not guilt-ridden perfectionists.

I (Mary) once took a hard hat and a set of architect's drawings along to a talk I gave, to make the point that there are usually several different people involved in the work on a building site. However, when it comes to home education, most of the tasks rest on the parents alone and this produces its own stresses. We are both the visionaries and the implementers who turn the vision into reality. It is hard to keep the overall vision in focus as well as deal with the day to day demands. Many times we could not see the wood for the trees and we found ourselves too absorbed with the details. It helped to make time to stand back, deliberately review what had been achieved and redefine the next set of goals.

Do we have to wait until the end of the road before seeing any reward for our investment? 'Yes and no' is the answer to that question. We will not know the final outcome for many years, but along the way we have seen indications of the way our children are turning out and how their thinking is developing. We have helped them to deal with their weaknesses of character as they arose. We have become better equipped to help them make decisions about work and subject choices in later life, as we came to know their abilities better. We have evaluated things with them as life unfolds. We have exposed them to the more unpleasant aspects of life at our own discretion, and discussed things with them when we felt they were ready. No one has imposed things upon us – we are the potters, they are the clay, in one sense. All these are aspects of the freedom we opted for by choosing Christian home education and not submitting to the world's values and system. This freedom is to be valued, but it has also cost us in an ongoing way. We have invested ourselves, we have cried and our hearts have ached for our own failings as much as for theirs, but in the end we will be able to look Jesus in the eye and tell him that we didn't leave the little ones in Egypt, even though Pharaoh pressed us to do so.

Condemning ourselves instead of valuing what we have got

I sometimes find myself stumbled by the sheer professionalism and jargon of all things relating to school, particularly with National Curriculum phraseology. 'How can I be achieving anything,' I ask myself, 'if I can't understand the teaching materials?' Or sometimes we feel that our attempts are very homespun and we always lack resources, because we can't afford them or we can't get hold of the proper equipment. At times like this we need the Lord to remind us that what he wants is a faithful people, not a sophisticated one. As long as we teach the children to the best of our ability and are not lazy in our efforts to make the material as interesting and informative as possible, then God will undertake for the rest.

We have come to realise that by comparison with the surrounding nations, Israel was a very simple and unsophisticated group. In fact they were expressly instructed to erect only basic altars, not elaborate temples which could easily become objects of idolatry in themselves. The difference between them and the other nations was that they were free to do what God wanted, to choose to obey him and to walk by faith. Sometimes we want to have the cake and eat it – that is, we want to have the resources and the security of being within the system, along with the spiritual freedom of being outside it. He has to remind us which we really value. We might find it difficult to be different from other people, but if we really subscribed to the system which would make us fit in and be the same, then our children would come out of the educational sausage machine with the mindset of Egypt imprinted on them. Do we really want that? The answer is, 'No', but if we want the product, then we have to pay for it.

How much does it cost?

'What's the price?' you may ask. Well, it has included some element of financial sacrifice, as local authorities were 'unable' to help home educating families with resources, despite the fact that their resources were saved by our children learning at home. And a home learning family is also more likely to be living on one income rather than two.

We felt the stigma of being non mainstream mentioned earlier (Hebrews 11:13–16, 24–27, 36–37 spring to mind here). Unfavourable reactions from grandparents and other family members are difficult to accept, although these can be short-lived and may often be resolved as objectors see good fruit being borne. And in some cases, members of the extended family can actually make a real and very valuable contribution to the whole home learning process.

There is also the element of the extra workload – we've been much busier and have had less free time to call our own. There are people in the house most of the time, so we have needed to consciously allow more time for our own relationship, so it didn't get swallowed up in the general activity in the home. Home learning is for the benefit of the children, but a home can sometimes slip into being child-centred as a result, rather than God-centred; if this occurs, it can easily produce selfish children. We also found the need to put a barrier round certain times or individual activities of our own, where possible, so as to maintain perspective. Because of the choices we made, we became aware that contemporaries and friends seemed to have a very different lifestyle. Our house got fuller as we collected resources and things that might be useful one day. It also has shown signs of wear and tear more quickly, as people are at home all day and lots of activity has taken place there. However, potentially there are more people to keep it in a good state of repair!

The children did not go out of the door for several hours each day for someone else to be responsible for them. We had the oversight of the whole of their lives – their learning, their leisure activities and free time, their friendships and so on. Great! – in one sense, and God has been more than willing to provide the resources for us to cope with that responsibility. However, it is possible for parents to feel daunted and overwhelmed by this, particularly in an age when children assume independence younger and younger, and responsibility for more aspects of a child's life is delegated away from the parents at an earlier and earlier age.

Conclusion

Christian home education is great. It provided us with many opportunities to fulfil our responsibilities as parents and communicate the Lord's ways to our children, as well as giving us the freedom to choose what they learn, when, how and who with. But it is also costly, and not for the faint-hearted or the double-minded. You don't have to be financially well off, because it can be carried out on a low budget. It's like Christian discipleship – the cost is not primarily in the area of money. It costs our time, the overhaul of our worldview and a major lifestyle change. It requires us to make a long term investment, by faith, into a vision that we will only see realised much further down the road. The cost cannot be known or categorised completely before embarking on the venture, but it's wise to make sure before the Lord that we understand something of it, before we set out. We know that he put it in our hearts, and so we had to go for it! As Peter said to Jesus, 'Where else shall we go, Lord? You have the words of eternal life'. Having seen that Christian education *is* ordinary education from the Lord's point of view, we could not choose the secular version until we felt relatively sure that our children were at an age and stage where they were mature enough to evaluate it for themselves and to stand firm in their faith.

Sharing Convictions and Living by Faith – a Father's View

- Martin and Carol Chamberlain
- Children – three sons and one daughter
- Age range between fourteen and twenty-one
- Living in Yorkshire
- Have always home educated

Deciding to home educate was certainly a shared decision for Carol and myself, but it was a fairly natural one as we had been involved in the discussions about Christian education which led to the establishment of Covenant Christian School in Stockport. Our vision was not only ideological. We wished to enjoy participating in the development of our children in what we felt would be a more natural environment, as well as one infused by a Christian ethos. In the home we felt less constrained to follow a structured approach than at a school; we were influenced by the freer Education Otherwise philosophy that prevailed at the time, expounded by some Christians too. I hope this article will show how our attitudes developed.

There's a story that Dick King-Smith tells about two geese in which the male always says, 'I quite agree dear'. As we set out to home educate I couldn't help feeling, at times, that I'd only got to accept the *idea*, as long as Carol was happy with the day-to-day commitment. I was in full-time employment and out of the house from 7.30 AM to 6.00 PM. However it wasn't long before I realised that my commitment could not be merely incidental.

Our vision for home education was not dimmed by moving away from Stockport or by the opposition of most of our closest friends. However, we have benefited enormously from the support of other home educating families and the growth of a Christian home education network, especially in the North West of England. We have had very little regular involvement with other local families, but we have been greatly blessed by attending once or twice yearly gatherings with other home educators. Carol's Christian mother and sister have been very supportive and good role models for our children. In all that we have done we have much to thank God for. We certainly feel convinced of the rightness of our decision; yet we wouldn't argue that it is a 'penny-in-the-slot' route to godliness for our children.

My role in the family system of education started as 'let's have fun' (and give Mum a break) up to about age twelve or so. Then things, for me, became more serious. I helped teach or organise GCSEs, firstly in biology, then art, geography, history and maths. Though Carol majored in the teaching of French and English, I still got involved in negotiating with exam centres, courses, and the like, for these subjects.

In the early years, we gave our children lots of freedom around a rough core curriculum of English, maths and later, French. For Bible studies or theology we enjoyed sitting together, usually in the early evening after tea, to share a book, an article or a missionary prayer letter or reading from a Bible passage, followed by prayer. These special times were also opportunities to think specifically of the needs of others as well as our own. It has been very encouraging to see how God has answered our prayers. We wish we'd kept a notebook to remember the answers we have received! In addition the children have been to various Christian camps and conferences and we see preaching and teaching as an important part of church life. We are nevertheless increasingly convinced of the importance of prayer and reading Scripture together as a family.

We believe that education at home has brought our children more intimately into the everyday affairs of our family. They were there when I came home one day, having been made redundant, and we prayed together. I will always remember their prayers; 'God is more important than work!' They were there when a new brother or sister arrived home. They were involved in visits to their granddad when he was dying of cancer, and deeply affected by his confession of faith just before he died. They saw us dealing with building renovations. They heard us pray about the choice of university for an elder brother. They knew of our concern for accommodation in another town for our second son, and witnessed how God answered wonderfully!

Of course all these things interrupted our plans and the regularity of our formal curriculum. Even though we would desire more discipline in this area we can certainly witness to God's help, for example, through the assistance of others, when things have gone 'wrong'. In the end, education in the home setting, does inevitably, have something of the wayside flavour of Deuteronomy 6. There is also lots of freedom for our children to explore their own interests. Our children have seen our involvement with other people through work and church commitments and have shared in their concerns.

Although, of course, education is not just about qualifications, in the remainder of this article I'll share something of the experience we gained through doing a range of exams as they were my particular responsibility as the children got older.

Considering that I'd never studied GCSE biology, art and history and never taught a GCSE maths class, how did we get into such a seemingly crazy endeavour? It's fair to say that other families who had successfully pioneered home education encouraged us, but we couldn't be sure that our experience would be as positive as theirs.

Biology was our first effort. We chose this as our 'compulsory science' as it seemed closest to our family's interests. We decided, for our own sanity as much as the children's, that we'd aim to take GCSEs over two or three years in no more than about five subjects. We began using a National Extension College (NEC) biology pack through another correspondence college, but without the tutorial support that they offered. In the early stages we took some advice from a friend. He explained some key biological principles and recommended a textbook. After this we acted largely independently and we followed the pack rather than the textbook. Gradually we realised the importance of planning activities according to the syllabus and setting out work for weeks ahead. The pack was fairly uninspiring and when we followed the syllabus a second time we were much more ready to use a variety of texts, following the example of another family. Through following others' advice we also became much better equipped with past papers, mark schemes and examiners' comments (available from the examination board). Between the first and second attempts the exam centres changed, though on both occasions the centres were over an hour's drive away and required three visits. We're about to start a third biology course, this time with a new IGCSE board. We still have no need to do practical examinations, but we need a whole new set of past papers and have to locate yet another exam centre.

As with all the GCSE work I'd done, I can remember times of pressure when I've had to mark and prepare work late at night. There was also the frustration of trying to understand what a question was driving at and how it would be marked. Our biologist friend helped us work out answers, but discovering exam board mark schemes was a great relief! Worse still was when my sons had to suffer convoluted answers and corrections from me because they were written late at night. They also often came without the benefit of face-to-face explanation, because I was usually at work when they read them. Yet all of them passed! Some would say that the C grade they received in the IGCSE was of greater value than an equivalent grade at GCSE, but for us success was enough and it was a great relief. The first exam success felt very much like a vindication of our home education policy.

On the two occasions we tackled geography GCSE, we followed similar lines to biology with the use of an NEC pack, but both times we used the tutorial support offered by the college. This experience was a positive one and the pack materials were good. Highlights, for me, were the exploration of water supply in a decision-making exercise and researching the geology of Mount St Helens, using the internet.

I had previously taught geography but had never felt comfortable with the fieldwork element of GCSE geography which in a local school had involved several teachers and 100 children invading Selby shopping centre. It was very different with one parent and one child researching a location, but I still found the fieldwork very time consuming and too prescriptive. This, according to the tutors who advised us, *was* the right way to do it. However, judging by the relatively poor results from our efforts I wonder if the tutors' advice was good. Nevertheless, the attendance of one of my sons at a local council meeting and his interview with a councillor, were a highlight of the fieldwork experience. On the second occasion, when interviewing for a questionnaire to investigate housing in diverse local communities, my son's developing interest in politics was revealed. In the end disappointing coursework was compensated for by some very good exam results. Both sons chose the human geography options in the exams, the exact opposite of the ones I would have chosen!

Our approach to history, a subject I had never studied at GCSE level, was perhaps the boldest. Steve Richards (educational director of NorthStarUK) recommended the IGCSE syllabus which best suited our situation and also my interests. This covered the Victorian era and the Second World War to modern times. The Victorian era is very relevant to West Yorkshire and I felt that it could give valuable insight into how Christians can influence society. There was a wealth of written and internet resources for the Victorian period, some of it very local. For example, a former curate at our local parish church is mentioned in John Pollock's book *Shaftesbury: The Poor Man's Earl*.

Although we set out to study history without an open learning pack and with no significant input from friends or a tutor, by the time we started we knew the best approach – follow the syllabus closely; obtain past papers and mark schemes, and choose a variety of textbooks. The mark scheme for IGCSE history was especially thorough and a great help. Choosing a variety of textbooks was right for this subject, though confusing in others. I discovered the Macmillan history series which was just right for our children. Very memorable for me were the insightful essays my boys wrote about the Bay of Pigs crisis (Cuba), which had been inspired by a book in this series. I enjoyed investigating our local Victorian history but, again, my sons' interests took off in a different direction, that of twentieth century history.

I was involved with art, maths and English at a different level, as we availed ourselves of courses at local Further Education colleges. These classes were with adults lasting for one year, and each one turned out to be a positive experience. For a long time I thought we'd never be able to do art GCSE with two of our children who were both clearly gifted in this subject. It seemed art didn't work 'by correspondence' and we had little idea how to teach it. Then we found out about a local adult evening class in GCSE art, so I enrolled with my two eldest sons, one of whom was only thirteen at the time. In just a few weeks I learnt a lot more than I had ever done at school. The class was in a neighbouring town thirty minutes drive away. Thus a whole evening was occupied, from arriving home from work then going straight out again. I really enjoyed the class, even though eventually I found that the homework was too demanding for me to continue. The art course, from mid-September to mid-June, did not just cover drawing, which was where our children's skills lay, but included lino cutting, printing and three-dimensional work as well.

The art exhibition at the end of the course coincided with my being made redundant. Consequently we suffered a serious drop in income. To cut a long story short, God provided for our needs through a variety of sources – for example an inheritance from a non-Christian aunt and support in French tuition, mainly through correspondence, from a home educating family who lived an hour and a quarter's drive away. Even the difficulty of redundancy was overruled by the establishment of a new role for me in the same organisation, which gave me much more time to devote to home education!

Maths was, we discovered rather later than we wished, a subject where one textbook using one method was a good idea. Because I enjoy maths I tended to revel in alternative explanations. The result could often be confusion for our not-very-mathematical children! Our first attempt at maths through a local college was so successful that we approached the subject too casually for our second son. By the time he came to study maths the staff had changed; the method of teaching became class based rather than one-to-one, and to our surprise the cost went up tenfold to £250. To cap it all, there was a staff change mid-year. For our third son we stuck to one textbook and went through the entire syllabus for a full year before he joined a class in a different college, repeating the same textbook. This course was for three hours one morning a week, for which we paid about £117 as he was under sixteen at the start and Further Education colleges are only funded for students aged sixteen and over.

As you may have gathered by now, once they were sixteen, our children went to study in a local sixth form. More could be said about this decision but it certainly wasn't the end of parental involvement. For example, between February and April, we made seven visits to various art colleges as far apart as Edinburgh (which we visited twice) and Bath, with various other places in between! It was great to feel so convinced that Edinburgh was the right place for our second lad and to find God opening the way for him to go there.

Reflecting now on our years of home education, what comments would I make?

- It involved more commitment than I've described or could ever have expected.
- At first we underestimated the importance of being involved together as a family, in prayerfully seeking solutions to issues as they arose.
- It was always a struggle to find time for home education.
- I needed to be bold enough and willing to venture into new things.
- I should have been more inclined to seek out as much advice as possible as early as possible.
- I needed to help enable my wife to fulfil what was for her, often a lead role. This meant social and church demands on time had to be carefully thought through, for the sake of our children's education.

Certainly the 'I quite agree dear' mentality that I mentioned at the beginning, was an inadequate reaction to the task of home education! I needed to hold to a conviction about the wisdom of our actions against those who would criticise or look askance at the way we were bringing up our children. Doing this thoughtfully and prayerfully was also important. After all, where does responsibility lie, if not with us as parents?

Finally, it's fair to say that in this adventure of faith we can say 'The LORD who delivered . . . will deliver' (1 Samuel 17:37) and we trust that, as Psalm 145:20 promises, he will continue to watch over us. God is good.

Joy and Grace

- James and Linda Hoyle
- Children – three girls and one boy
- Age range between two and thirteen
- Living in West Yorkshire
- Have home educated for seven years

Home education began for us as though we were looking through a keyhole. We spent a long time gazing through from the other side contemplating how exciting it all looked. When we finally turned the key, made the decision, and walked in to the home education arena it was far better than we had dared to imagine and the door back to where we had come from soon became overgrown and lost and never once looked for amongst all the good things God gave us. That initial decision which had involved hostility and misunderstanding from people became a deeply grounded conviction and we soon found that, through a choice to home educate our children, there were now many more keyholes that we seemed to be gazing through. God works thoroughly and sometimes, it appears, slowly. But he is gracious and as when we first came to Christ we were babes in our faith he still gently leads us on the way we should go.

When we were first introduced to the idea of home schooling one of the main things that repeatedly put us off was the fact that everyone we ever spoke to who was home schooling appeared to have loads of children or at least more than we had. They also managed to get up a lot earlier in the morning than we did! In fact I think they still do. We foolishly felt that perhaps with two children home education would somehow just not work.

At the time we had Daniel who was six and Rosanna who was four. We had withdrawn Daniel from school just as Rosanna was due to begin. Although we had heard of the concept of home education nearly two years previously it had taken time for God to work thoroughly in us both so that together we had a strong conviction that this was what God had called our family to do. In light of some of the teething problems such as family members struggling with and vehemently opposing our choice we could see God's hand at work in those years of preparation. That first year we mixed and matched various books of curriculum and learned with our children what phonics were, alongside settling down to a more flexible lifestyle – one not dominated by school times. This flexibility was particularly appreciated as Jamie has always worked shifts, making weekend events of any kind not always manageable. We still remember, that first autumn, taking our children to a favourite park and walking in the afternoon with not a soul in sight! Hesitantly Daniel would ask whether all the other children had finished school yet, as though we were doing something dreadfully naughty. No they hadn't and wasn't this great?

Both our children had been delivered by caesarean section and with each there had been complications. So, after taking medical advice at the time, we were advised not to have more children. Discussing the options and ironically bearing in mind my youth at the time (twenty-one when Rosanna arrived); we decided that Jamie would have a vasectomy.

Looking back we feel that the decision was the right one and that God knew our reasons and motives. He would also know that through that decision he would show himself more clearly and work a miracle in our lives.

As our children grew, our desire for another child grew also. Over the years before we came to home education, we explored repeatedly how Jamie's vasectomy could be reversed. Time and time again it was explained to us that it would be costly and the likelihood that it would actually be successful was very low. It would need to be done privately and we were advised that the surgeon would be unlikely to be sympathetic to our desire to have more children. With no ready cash it was constantly dismissed but never quite let go of. So we come to another conundrum we found in home educating families. They often had large numbers of children who were born many years apart! We did not know anyone who had anything other than two or three children neatly scheduled in to life or perhaps Mum's maternity leave. Family and friends had encouraged us in our choice to limit the size of our family but with the passing of time we believed we had limited it too severely.

Soon after our home education adventure began we started exploring the idea of a home business. Due to this we often received complimentary magazines from the United States on family life, with relevance to home education specifically. Flicking through the advertisements at the back of an old copy of *Homeschooling Today* our eyes were caught by a tiny advert with the header, 'Has God changed your heart regarding the size of your family?' Our answer was, 'Most definitely yes'. The advert gave the briefest of details about a doctor in Texas who performed microscopic vasectomy reversals at what appeared to be a very reasonable cost. Though my heart was already jumping ahead and deciding on names for the baby, Jamie was a little more down to earth, noting that Texas was a very long way away and surely would prove expensive to get to. As Jamie rang the given telephone number I searched the Internet for flights.

Four weeks later Jamie found himself on an international flight bound for Atlanta. He flew on to San Antonio in Texas where he picked up a rental vehicle and drove to New Braufnels to meet Doctor Cary Leverett. God truly does work in amazing ways his wonders to perform. There was no doubt in our minds that if Jamie boarded that plane we would have another child. At that time God had put on our hearts a verse from the gospel of Mark: Chapter nine verse twenty-three reads, 'If thou canst believe, all things are possible to him that believeth' (KJV). The verse is a response Jesus makes to a man who is pleading for him to heal his son. The man replies, 'Lord, I believe; help thou mine unbelief.' It was a giant leap of faith for Jamie to travel to Texas to meet a man we had never met and who would then perform delicate surgery, with such hope bound up in it. At that period in our lives, when events were moving so fast it was at times frightening; but God graciously gave us an abundance of faith alongside a deep sense of peace.

Dr. Leverett performs numerous reversals and his whole ministry is geared towards helping families have more children, in particular home educating ones like ours who would most probably have the restriction of one income. Able to afford to cover all the costs it was cheaper to fly Jamie to New Braufnels and have the private surgery there, than to follow the private path in this country.

Jamie met Dr. Leverett for the first time the morning he had arrived at a local motel. Dr. Leverett spent time in prayer with him, going on to explain that due to the original surgery having been done just less than five years prior to the planned reversal, he was certain that bar any other reasons we would be blessed with more children. On the walls in the room where the surgery is performed are numerous pictures of babies and young children all born as a result of the parents visiting Dr. Leverett. On the majority of occasions both parents are able to visit Doctor Leverett; however as

Jamie had travelled alone from abroad he was welcomed in to Doctor Leverett's family. He was warmly treated to meals out where he enjoyed true fellowship. He was much encouraged in our home educating adventure, returning home with armfuls of home education magazines.

Three months later we were expecting a baby, affectionately known as Tex throughout the pregnancy. Our amazed doctor was eager to help us in our quest to avoid more caesarean surgery. However when Daniel was eight-and-a-half and Rosanna nearly seven, Elizabeth Joy was born, delivered by caesarean. We gave her the name Elizabeth meaning 'God is my oath', as we believed that God had promised us a child when we took a step of faith in what can only be described as a mountain top experience. In the Bible, Elizabeth had been barren but God gave her a child; and when we learned Doctor Leverett had a daughter called Elizabeth this helped confirm her choice of name. We also named her Joy because from the moment we expected her arrival, joy was the overriding emotion we felt. Psalm 113:9 says, 'He maketh the barren woman to keep house, and to be a joyful mother of children.'(KJV). Pregnancy and birth are of God exclusively and though sometimes they are withheld according to his will when they do happen it is a blessing from him. Her names serve as a constant reminder to us of what God has done.

This whole experience happened early in our adventure in home education and was such an amazing testimony and confirmation for us. The whole experience revolving around Elizabeth's conception and birth was a time when our faith grew and was strengthened. Our conviction to home educate our children became stronger and our hearts were turned anew back to them.

Repeatedly in the books of the Bible God's people are reminded to look back and remember what God has done for them and not to forget his grace and mercy towards them. In difficult times it is good to look back and see what God has done for us and to remember his faithfulness. You cannot stay on the mountain.

Maintaining the home education of our older children throughout my pregnancy with Elizabeth was never a problem and when she arrived we seemed to easily continue the pattern, as she was a happy baby. However, when the fourth pregnancy began home education became more challenging. This time the whole pregnancy was fraught with problems and at the same time we appeared to move from one major dilemma to another. From the beginning of the pregnancy there were concerns over the baby's health, ultimately whether the baby would survive and if it did what problems it might have. At twenty-four weeks we were shocked to find ourselves being offered an abortion due to the high risk of possible complications. Throughout the pregnancy we dealt with the deaths of both friends and family, serious illnesses, disputes, and work and family problems. This time it was anything but joy!

Alongside the concerns over the baby's health I was generally unwell throughout and a hospital stay at one point nearly delivered a premature baby. With a one-year-old now tottering around and Jamie out for long and unsociable hours it was a real struggle to get through a day let alone teach academics. We had always liked the unit study approach and so made use of this, though Daniel and Rosanna still kept on with their own core subjects. After our concerns about the age gap between the children this was often proved to be a blessing, as the older ones clearly were quite independent and increasingly helpful around the house.

Rachel Grace was delivered by caesarean section just two years after Elizabeth's arrival. Healthy and content we gave her the name Rachel, as she was much loved as was the wife of Jacob, and Grace as only by God's grace did we get through those incredibly testing months. As James 1:2–3 says, 'Consider it pure joy, my brothers, whenever you face trials of many kinds, because you know that the testing of your faith develops perseverance' (KJV). On occasions it appeared too easy for us to forget the joy and certainly not count it pure joy, and to sinfully grumble against God about our trials. In the future we will always be able to look back to that special time of grace, telling again of God's amazing love reminding us to ever keep our eyes fixed on Christ. The contrasting pregnancies serve only to show us how God has always used times of suffering to show how his grace is all sufficient and to help us get our priorities in order.

The way we continued home educating changed again as Rachel joined the family. At one time we would give Daniel and Rosanna a sheet of tasks on a Monday morning, for the week. This proved a good system as less time was spent asking what they should be doing next and it helped to ensure that at least a minimum amount of both academic and household work was finished each week. I would review and redo the sheets on a Friday evening. We also posted extra jobs, with terms of employment, for them where they could earn money whilst being of practical help.

Clearly, educating one child at home is a full-time job and with the various ages, subjects and interests of four children it was and can still be a real challenge. At times we are aware of the age gap and it did feel a difficult task to meet the needs of the two older children with those of a toddler and baby. Practically, actually teaching them could be chaos and I found myself becoming increasingly a picture of a caricature home-school mum: baby on one knee, toddler whining, ten-year-old not in the mood for maths, an older one asking probing questions and that never-ending pile of ironing. I would then stir in a good dose of bedtime blues when I would woefully consider all I had not managed to achieve!

Some of the stresses and pressures of this time were unavoidable; however the home education remained constant and our conviction to continue never wavered, despite adding up after an exhausting day, how many years were left! Sometimes the home education felt like a side issue, something we did in our spare time. Elisabeth Elliot tells us that 'a choice is a limitation' and this is something we had to learn to appreciate. Home educators frequently mention that the degree of flexibility is a big benefit of having the children home all day. But we can forget this and perhaps due to unseen pressures to conform to a pattern of home education, we do not always make the best use of it. We do believe that it is important that our children have a good academic education, but we also know that our priority is that one day our children will stand with us in heaven.

We have learnt now that home education does not need a particular number of children and that we should test and confront the world's ways, examine them and return to the Lord. Within the names Rachel and Grace is the word race reminding us to run with patience (or perseverance) the race that is set before us (Hebrews 12:1).

So if you ever find yourself sitting in our house with a hot tea in a 'Texas' mug you'll know why!

May God's word be our joy, our comfort and our encouragement.

Ebenezer; So Far Has the Lord Helped Us

- David and Colette Harding
- Children – two boys
- Aged twenty and twenty-seven
- David and Colette live in North East Manchester
- Always home educated

When I was first contemplating motherhood, I was lent some wonderfully inspirational books. They produced in me an ideal to seek to bring up my children, as if I was bringing up the Lord (Colossians 3:23), whilst still recognising that both my children and I were sinners. We are told in Scripture to do all things 'to the glory of God' (Colossians 3:17; 1 Corinthians 10:31). Causing little ones to turn away from believing in Christ was a very serious offence (Matthew 18:6; Mark 9:42). We resolved to try to have a home which would be free of anything that might hinder our children's and our own spiritual progress.

Talking with older Christian women, I was astounded at how many said that all children will naturally rebel against parents when they reach their teens. There was nothing we could do; it was just a phase they all passed through. If we were 'lucky', then it wouldn't be permanent, but if it was, then you just had to pray that the Lord would bring them back. This didn't seem to fit with the principles I had seen in Scripture, that we should train our children in godliness, *expecting* them to follow the Lord, and warning them of the seriousness of turning away from the truth. It seemed to me that the Lord gave us the responsibility to maintain a godly home and that we were to trust him to work in their lives to bring them to salvation. Our children are *born* rebels. It is not something that suddenly develops in teenagers. We have all those early years to help them see their condition, and seek God's mercy and grace.

The first major challenge as to how we would apply these lofty ideals, came when I was pregnant with our first child and was supply teaching in a local primary school. I was not happy with what I saw school doing to young children. Also I was not happy with how they left that primary school educationally, often with low levels of literacy. As Christians, we were also well aware of the great conflict of cultures that we knew existed between our lifestyle and that promoted at school, either by peers or professionals. In books, this included evolution presented as fact, the frequent references to magic in stories, and naughtiness being portrayed as amusing or fun. The children's creative writing and times of play together seemed largely limited to what they had seen on television, particularly the fighting programmes for the boys. Bad language, particularly misusing the Lord's name, was normal among the juniors. Young children coming into school soon modified their own behaviour to survive in their new environment. We felt very uneasy at the thought of placing our child, entrusted to us by God to bring up to know and love him, into such a place. And, educationally, I could surely do better myself.

Home education was not something that had ever entered my head back in the late 1970s. Very few were doing it at all, even fewer for Christian reasons. Eventually we were put in touch with a couple of other families with similar persuasions to ours and we met them when our son was ten months old. We stayed with Mike and Jan Matthews and also spent time with Roy and Jean Mohon nearby, who had produced their own material for educating their children. They helped us think things through more thoroughly, and biblically. They encouraged us to make reasonable preparations; in our own minds as much as anything else.

After spending a weekend with these two families, we felt like we needed to re-educate ourselves about our whole way of thinking. We heard for the first time, the phrase 'a Christian worldview', and came to see that so many of us compartmentalise life into work, family, church, or school settings, failing to see that the Lord is Lord over all these areas. The fact that the Bible is equally relevant to every part of life was not something we had heard before . . . mainly because from childhood we were trained in humanistic thinking. We absorb that worldview without realising it. At teacher training college I had thought I had taken uncompromising stands because I had lived a certain lifestyle. But my ways of thinking had been affected by all the godless instruction I had come under. It was easy to apply faith to my moral life, and leave it out of my intellectual life, as if it had no application there. These dear friends opened our eyes to the dual standards we were used to. As we began to read more about Christian education in one book by Roy Mohon, and others by American authors, we began to understand the issues more clearly.

No Christians we knew would ever have asked a liberal, let alone an atheist, to come and instruct their adult congregation on a Sunday. Yet every day, those same Christians would send their children to be taught by godless people. Arguments could be made that it might be a 'church' school, or in a 'nice' (i.e. middle class) area, and not too bad. The teacher may be a 'lovely' lady. On the other hand the teacher may be immoral or dishonest. There would be nothing a parent could do about it. Either way, most teachers were strangers to the gospel of Christ, and could never help our children in the one thing that mattered most. Indeed, by teaching our children that they had to fit in with a school system where what they heard at home or church didn't always apply, we ourselves would be hindering their spiritual progress. We thought that these things were so obvious now, it wouldn't be long before the majority of believers in this country must surely begin setting up Christian schools. If we wanted our children to trust Christ while young and go on to walk in his ways, they needed training in righteousness by those who love the word of God. To encourage our own church to consider Christian education as an important issue, we even had an American representative come and address a small group of us. We could not believe the apathy with which the idea was met.

Meanwhile, I had to think about how I would set out on this venture on a day-to-day basis. Knowing how learning is such fun to little ones, I tried introducing my son to words very early on and he loved it. He was soon in a routine where he looked forward to spending part of each morning at the table with me drawing, painting, writing or doing numbers. Part of each day would be spent learning about God and how we fit into His world. We used *Leading Little Ones to God* by Marian Schoolland, as a basis for this at first. Normal family life, outings and things we found in the garden, all became a starting point for learning and exploring together. We made our own little books filled with drawings, pictures cut from magazines, photographs and relevant words.

He took to it so well that he was reading fluently by four. This gave *me* the needed confidence to boldly let others know that Matthew would not be going to school, at least for the primary years, for which I was trained and knew I could manage. I lost a friend or two amongst my neighbours for this bizarre announcement and my father disowned me (for a couple of years) saying he no longer had an elder daughter, and that he would 'report me to Social Services'. Since we were at that time fostering through Social Services, I did not feel unduly threatened by that, but I did keenly feel his personal antipathy. My parents were divorced; my mother approved enthusiastically of our decision, because she knew how bad the behaviour was in schools in her area, so that was some consolation. Neither of my parents lived nearby anyway.

We did have concerns that for seven years Matthew was an only child. During this time we were fostering, which gave some close contact with other children, but no stability in relationships. Church and sports clubs made up for some of this, and playing with neighbours added to his mixing. He always found it very easy to get alongside people of all ages. We also had an open home for international students; Matthew had great patience in listening to their broken English and showing interest in their concerns. His academic work was fine and he was learning to play the piano from me.

When Matthew was seven, after many miscarriages, our second child arrived much to his delight. They would be a 'whole school apart' in their studies, with Joel being primary age just as Matthew would be the age to start secondary school, but they were thrilled to be able to do their learning alongside each other.

At eleven or twelve Matthew had begun having free violin lessons at the local middle school, and was playing in their small orchestra. This had given him a glimpse of school life, and the facilities available to children of his age. I was not sure how I would cope with secondary levels of learning, but was still reluctant to hand him over to godless strangers to influence his life from then on. However, we did ask Matthew if he would like to try attending school. His answer was such an encouragement to us. He had not liked what he had seen of the way large numbers of children act when all together in a school environment. He already had one girl in particular saying she wanted to 'go out with him' (at the age of twelve). He had no desire to spend seven hours a day, five days a week in such a setting, and would far rather continue learning at home. This filled him and us with a real resolve to make it work, whatever time, effort and cost was going to be required.

By now Matthew had an unusual love of numbers, data, timetables, and suchlike. All his free time seemed taken up with recording endless lists of calculations. It used to exasperate me as I couldn't see any value in the hours he spent on such things. It was obviously just the way his mind worked and an essential approach for the type of work he now does, in aircraft design and testing. He was able to pursue this even more as computers developed and he bought himself software which taught flying skills along with fuel planning and other such technicalities. He knew he wanted to work with aircraft.

As GCSE age loomed, I felt I needed a taste of what was required and so I enrolled at night class in a subject I was doing with the boys but had been 'thrown out of' at school because I was so hopeless – Spanish. Wouldn't my old teacher have been amazed to see the A-grade certificate I got! At this time, we were preparing to move from rural Bedfordshire to an industrial, deprived area in the north of England. We decided Matthew should begin three non essential subjects to take a year earlier than normal, studying them in one year instead of two. We chose electronics, human biology and computer studies, all with correspondence colleges (National Extension College and Rapid Results College). We moved just in time to find a centre in Manchester where he could sit the exams and his good grades were a relief and encouragement to us.

The following year he took history, maths, English, Spanish and physics. At this time Further Education colleges were allowed to take in under sixteens; so it cost us nothing and he did two subjects at night class, and three subjects on a flexi-learning approach. He also did practical evening courses in car maintenance and woodwork that year. He then went on to do physics, maths and business studies A levels at the college. It always amazed him that even at that stage of non-compulsory A levels, the majority of students didn't bother doing their assignments or turning up regularly for lessons.

His grades earned him an offer from his first choice university, University of Manchester Institute of Science and Technology (UMIST). We had convictions against going into debt to attend university, so he would be able to live at home and travel in each day by train. He then took a year out, through the Year in Industry scheme. He was placed at an engineering firm across the road from our house and during the year earned a National Examining board in supervisory Management (NEBSM) certificate by doing three residential weeks of training at Pershore College. These weeks were his first experience of living away from home with non-Christians. Sharing a room with a lad the same age who was so drunk he was sick when he arrived back in the early hours of the morning, helped Matthew to see first-hand the contrast between his own choices of lifestyle and those of others he met, who didn't know the Lord. He won an award from The Year in Industry scheme for a presentation he made at an engineering exhibition during his time there. We felt so grateful to the Lord for his provision of an excellent university course nearby and for the opportunity to earn at a local firm for a year. Our move to the north had proved part of God's plan for our children as well as for David's job as a pastor.

By the time he started university, he was confident of his abilities, had experience in the world of work and worked well with teams whether of peers or older colleagues. In the first term, his team won an award for their working design of an aeroplane wing. In his last eighteen months at UMIST, he found himself work placements with the Air Accident Investigation Branch in Farnborough and for six months with British Airways at Heathrow working on their flight data recording systems.

He graduated in 2002 and has since been working with BAE Systems and then Spirit AeroSystems. This has included over six months working in Seattle alongside Boeing engineers. It is a great privilege for him to be able to work in the subject he has always enjoyed so much. He is also walking in the life principles we have shared with him, which is obviously the most important thing to us. He recently married a lovely Christian girl from the USA and they have already decided to home educate any children they may have in the future.

Our second son, Joel, was not so single-minded in his approach. He too learned to read before he was four. He always had an incredible way with words and loved making puns as soon as he knew that some words had more than one meaning. He was also very good with maths, but didn't want to spend his life using it. He too learned piano from me and has a good ear for music, being able to harmonise from the age of about seven when we sang together as a family. At eight he also began the trumpet, and showed a lot of skill in this. By the time he was nine he was in the local youth orchestra and doing well in music exams. His interest in history was also apparent early on, knowing a great deal about various soldiers and battles through the ages and having a good memory for details.

During ten years of Joel's life, his closest auntie suffered from cancer. She lived in Canada, and since I had to go out a few times to care for her, Joel also accompanied me on some of those trips. It was wonderful having the flexibility to take him and his studies with us as we travelled. My sister appreciated having him around. I didn't feel that he was being neglected, and of course Joel absolutely loved it!

We didn't know what he would want to do career wise and neither did he. As with his brother, we started on three GCSEs a year early. These were accounting, human physiology/health and music, again using National Extension College courses. Studying music had introduced him to writing his own compositions, which he much enjoyed.

The following year he took maths, history and English. Also, a Christian home educating friend who taught languages did Spanish with him and a few other home educated children (in seven months, and all got good grades). He did music A level a year early at the school where he had been an external candidate for GCSE. They agreed to him going into the sixth form for music lessons only, despite being younger than the others in the class.

We did wonder about him trying for Chethams, the specialist music school in Manchester. However, we decided that this would have contradicted our principles about putting him, too young, into an environment where the Lord was not loved, and personal success came first. Instead, he auditioned for a place at the Royal Northern College of Music Junior School and was successful. This meant that all day Saturday would be given over to tuition at the college in Manchester. Joel's involvement in two orchestras, rehearsing two nights a week and in various activities at church meant his time was filled up. The normal school route of eight to ten GCSEs taken all at once would have been unnecessary pressure. He was glad to be able to do things at his pace and give priority to what he thought was important.

He then did two further A levels; classical civilisation and business studies as correspondence courses. Since he had completed music early, he was now only doing two subjects but with his extra music commitments, found this was quite enough. We enjoyed having a 'laid-back' year, travelling around to see various classical civilisation sites, or fitting in revision around household decorating jobs and suchlike.

For higher study, Joel was offered two unconditional places at conservatoires, and he chose to go to Glasgow's Royal Scottish Academy of Music and Drama (RSAMD). His main subject is composition and second study, trumpet. He is now there enjoying it a great deal. Again he feels privileged to have been able to study his own choices, at his own pace and to be training for a career in something he really loves doing. He too is a Christian and wants to live in a way consistent with his beliefs. Studying in the arts inevitably brings various conflicts and already he has had to choose to take a stand on a number of issues. The pressures that are put on young people nowadays to cast aside their parents' standards is immense. We are so grateful to God that he enabled us to bring up our children in this way training them, to the best of our ability, to have a Christian worldview which does affect the decisions they make and guide them in a way which leads to life.

One of the 'potential problems' posed to us by well meaning friends, was our own lack of expertise in certain areas. How could we teach our children those things which we ourselves were not skilled in? Examples cited were maths, physics and music. Funnily enough these were the two areas Matthew and Joel have gone on to specialise in. Having been in the bottom maths division when I was at school, I knew my great limitations. But once children have a love for learning and are interested in something, motivation makes up for any lack of expertise on the part of the parents. And our God is in control. Little did we realise when we moved near to Manchester, how useful that would be in providing for both our children's educational needs.

Wanting our boys to feel pleased with what they had accomplished, but to remind them it was only through the Lord's help, we decided to present them with awards at the times they would have left primary and secondary school. They were engraved with their names and the reason for the award, and a specially chosen Bible verse. We called these the Ebenezer trophies, like the stone set up by Samuel in 1 Samuel 7:12 and both boys appreciated receiving these.

We know we did not do everything right. If we were starting out again, we would probably try to include more character training, using some of the excellent material which is now available, as much for ourselves as for our children! Bible memorisation is also more important than we gave time for. It was certainly well worth doing our history projects going right back to Genesis. We enjoyed making a colourful scroll for each of the great civilisations and adorning our walls with them. These were wonderful in showing us where we fit into the big scheme of things. To learn how God has had his hand in all of history, the rise and fall of nations, the preparation for the coming of the Lord Jesus Christ and the growth and suffering of the church through the centuries, has been invaluable to our whole family. What confidence it gives in trusting him for all the little details of our lives!

Looking back we are glad that we did what we could, within the limitations of our attempting things almost from scratch. Thanks must go to those who advised us in those early days. We trust that God will help our boys to build on this foundation and make greater progress, by starting out further on than either of us were, when we set out on the adventure of raising godly offspring for him. And may he be pleased to bless the efforts of all families seeking to do the same.

Six Into
Thirty-four Will Go!

- Jonathan and Jill Hawken
- Children – two boys and two girls
- Age range between thirteen and eighteen
- Living in Gloucestershire
- Have home educated for fourteen years

Looking back, it seems that our home educating experience began when we attended the first ever UK Christian home school conference at Cliff College in 1992. We were both familiar with the college as Jonathan and I met on a United Beach Missions team and the annual reunions of beach missions were also held at Cliff College, in the days when there was frost on the inside of the dormitory windows! Matthew was born in Suffolk but shortly afterwards we moved to Wantage (Oxfordshire) where Daniel, Rosemary and Heather were born. When I had Rosemary I met an American friend who intended to home school her children and I think that she was our first introduction to the idea. I don't remember how we found out about the conference but we decided we would leave the children with my parents in North Staffordshire and go along to look and learn. At this time Matthew was just four, Daniel was three, Rosemary only one and I was expecting Heather. We came away thinking that if our children developed in the same mould as the ones we saw there (the older children in particular) we

189

would be grateful. As I write the children are eighteen, seventeen, fifteen and thirteen, and we are truly thankful for God's guidance and faithfulness over the intervening years. The visiting Canadian speaker at the conference was a real inspiration and it was great to meet with people who we now realise were at the forefront of Christian home education in the UK. We all owe a lot to them.

At this time (1992) Jonathan's job was about to change. He worked in the electricity industry near Wantage and he was about to be moved either to a power station or to the headquarters in Gloucester. If Matthew had gone to the local village school we knew he would be moving within the first year. At this point all the children had afternoon naps. The thought of waking two children and a new-born and walking twenty minutes to the school, in January, was more than I could imagine, so we took the plunge and said Matthew would stay at home with me until we had moved and were settled. I think in our hearts we knew that he and Daniel would not be going to school in the near future but we just said we were taking things 'one term at a time'. Both boys attended the village playgroup two mornings a week and they were allowed to continue until we moved; around Matthew's sixth birthday as it happened. The playgroup leader was very supportive and fed Matthew an endless stream of books to read, which he devoured. Daniel showed no such inclinations and has always been happier doing it rather than reading about it. Shortly before we moved to Gloucester, Matthew learned to ride his bike and asked me to fasten the top of a music stand onto the handlebars in order that he could carry on reading the Narnia series whilst pedalling round the yard! I persuaded him that this was not a good idea and that he could sing instead. This was also Matthew's first experience of that awful feeling of nearing the end of an excellent book and wondering '. . .whether I will ever find anything as good to follow it'. As he realised that he was reading the last Narnia book, he decided he would write the eighth so as to have something to go on to. There was the difficulty that he couldn't yet write and so he dictated it to me. It was called *The Next Adventure* and we got through several pages of an exercise book before Ransome's *Swallows and Amazons* came along to claim his attention.

We settled down north of Gloucester and went to an Open Brethren church in Newent. We were, and still remain, the only home educating family in the church. On Sundays Jonathan would do our family 'Bible time' and then we all went to the morning Breaking of Bread service.

Daniel, Rosemary and Heather all spent some time in the village playgroup. Daniel and Rosemary were learning to read using Ladybird books and an American set of readers called *Making New Friends*. These readers came with workbooks that we also used. Daniel found reading quite difficult and spelling almost impossible – now at age sixteen he has been diagnosed with dyslexia. He has always been the practical sort and the boys spent hours building train tracks and marble runs, and floating table tennis balls in the stream after it had rained. He was always asking for wood to build things with, but he stumped me during a rocket project when he came running in to ask me if I had 'just a little bit of dynamite in the cupboard'!

Another interest, which has since developed into a major involvement for us all, was music. Daniel had been asking to play the violin so I made a few enquires about Suzuki beginner groups but they were too far to travel to. I then saw a poster advertising a children's music group for singing, recorders and string playing just a short drive away. This group had started when a musical family taught their own children and a few other friends, on a Saturday morning in their kitchen. Over about ten years they had expanded to various outbuildings in the large garden. We began to join in with singing and recorders and shortly afterwards Daniel started to learn the violin and Matthew the cello. As the girls reached the age of four or five they started to join in on eighth-size violins. The parents were welcomed and encouraged to sit in the group lessons and orchestras and to help with practice at home. I found it was very tricky to get my hands around Daniel's quarter-size violin so we dug Jonathan's old school violin from the loft and I started to join in too. This music group and their church friends formed the basis of the children's 'socialisation'. They have all progressed through the music grades on strings and piano with oboe for Matthew, tenor sax for Daniel, singing for Rosemary and bassoon for Heather, all making recent appearances.

We had contact with a Gloucester based group of home educating families who met once a week for singing, French and pottery. It was not a Christian group but everyone was extremely supportive and we all valued each other. I learned a lot watching others and the children enjoyed the friendships and activities. The group met for about four years and dissolved as we all went our separate ways.

Over the years we had often talked about the possibility of travelling around Europe in a motorhome for a year or so. At some point this changed to North America. Originally we had thought that we would need to return in time for Matthew to start secondary school. As the years had passed and our home educating had definitely become conviction rather than convenience we knew that Matthew did not need to go to secondary school. When we first talked about an extended trip abroad we had thought that Jonathan would resign from work. Looking back we realise this would not have worked financially and in God's timing he was able to take redundancy from work. We sold our house in one weekend to Matthew's cello teacher and in February 1999 we flew out to Orlando in Florida where we rented a house for a month while we looked around for a large motorhome or Recreational Vehicle (RV) as the Americans call them. We had a lot of different reactions to the trip. These included, 'How will you cope all day every day with six of you in a box?' (thirty-four foot by eight foot six, in fact.) My father told us, 'Go while you can and enjoy yourselves' while another said, 'I wouldn't do that; you are very brave'. I don't think we felt brave, just slightly nervous and extremely fortunate to have the health and strength to do it.

We found a suitable second-hand RV and being cash buyers last thing on a Saturday afternoon, got the deal we wanted. For anyone interested, it was an Itasca Suncruiser made by Winnebago. It had a ninety-four gallon tank and a Cummins diesel engine, which was under the double bed at the back (a 'diesel pusher'). With the rear view camera, cruise control and of course, an automatic gearbox, it was a treat to drive. Jonathan loved it but I managed a circuit of a large, empty car park and left it at that.

We had a rough plan of places to visit in the first six months, including a return to the UK for a month. There were several reasons for this. The first was that there was a total solar eclipse in Cornwall in August 1999 and Jonathan had been interested in that for years. Also, if the trip was not being as successful as we had hoped, we could admit it and return home then. It also meant we could renew visas and show the grandparents that the children were alive and thriving, even if they did have temporary American accents and used a few funny phrases. Heather picked up such an accent that I overheard her talking to someone in a swimming pool and didn't realise it was her speaking until I looked.

Leaving Orlando, we travelled to the Gulf Coast and through Alabama to Louisiana and New Orleans. We then headed northeast to the sea, travelling up the South and North Carolina coasts visiting islands called The Outer Banks. By June we were in New York State and visited New York City on our one and only organised tour. It was the only city Jonathan didn't drive through in the RV, which turned out to be a wise move when we saw just how busy it really was.

We had home schooling friends in Michigan (whom we had met in the Gloucester home education group), so we headed across Pennsylvania and Ohio, staying on Amish-run campgrounds. Home schooling is so popular in the USA that there was no need to explain what we were doing as people just assumed it anyway. After visiting our friends, we headed back south to Florida and, leaving the RV on a campground, flew home for a month. We saw the eclipse and the grandparents, ate Cadbury's chocolate and then returned to collect our RV and head off west again; just in time to avoid a hurricane which had also decided to arrive in Florida.

Jonathan particularly wanted to visit the annual Confederate Airforce Show in Texas, so that was our next focus. We saw all the old aircraft and Jonathan and the boys climbed all over them before we watched an amazing glider display at night. The planes were all lit up and the aerobatics were accompanied by music and fireworks, launched from the gliders' wingtips.

Our 'RV schooling' took place at various times depending on the schedule for the day. If we were staying on the campground the books would come out in the morning before it got too hot. Daniel, Rosemary and Heather were still reading out loud to us and Jonathan took on the listening. They usually sat on our double bed in the separate room at the rear of the RV. Finding books for ourselves and Matthew to read was a continuing problem. We had very limited storage space so books were a luxury. We bought quite a few for the children while we made do with the 'take a book, leave a book' system that operated on a lot of campgrounds. We took out quite a lot of Lego and Playmobil and these, along with the small zoo of furry animals that they accumulated, kept the children occupied for hours. Fortunately, they all played well together and had to be each other's friends in the absence of anyone else. We went through a good range of bedtime stories, including the whole of the *Little House on the Prairie* series; while we travelled through North Dakota and Arkansas later on in the trip. The RV had a video monitor which we used to watch a few of the *Veggietales* videos. If you have never seen these, you'll just have to imagine a tomato and a cucumber acting out Bible stories.

The children rapidly became connoisseurs of campgrounds. They studied the maps given to us upon check-in and were off to the playground before we had the hydraulic jacks down. Campgrounds without a swimming pool were definitely second best. They all learnt to swim like fish and could almost beat us at swimming races.

We travelled through New Mexico and Arizona before arriving in California in mid-December. In New Mexico we camped at Red Rock for the hot air balloon festival. Next door to us happened to be the couple who were ground crew for one of the balloons. We were all pleased to be offered flights over the desert. They started at about 7.00 AM when it was dark and *cold*. It was 0° F, the coldest we experienced and the only time the RV's water pipes froze. Another time when we experienced the kindness of the people we met was at Thanksgiving in November. We were staying near Las Vegas at the time, in Nevada. A local church sent a few people to the large campground each Sunday to have a service for the campers. When they realised that we were thousands of miles from our families for Thanksgiving Day they invited us to the church celebration so we could sample turkey and pumpkin pie.

In Arizona we had some fascinating desert walks amongst the 'hands-up cactus' as Daniel called the saguaros. We also went to the Grand Canyon, managing to get to the North Rim before they closed the road for the winter and found ourselves to be the only ones camping in the woods. The trails down into the canyon are from the south side so we made our way round and set off about 7.00 AM one morning when the mules left with their riders. We walked down for several hours – it gets hotter and hotter as you descend. It is possible to walk to the Colorado River and stay there overnight but this was too much for the children (and very expensive). We returned up the well-worn sandy track and got back just as the mules arrived home from their day. We were amused to see that we were in better shape than those who had spent the day in the saddle. The mules choose to walk on the outer edge of the path and it's a long way down when you peer over.

We had wondered about attending a home school conference but we were never in the right place at the right time. We didn't have Internet access except at a few campgrounds and at that time none of our relatives had email, so our post was all forwarded from the friends in Michigan. We finally arrived at the Pacific Coast about a week before Christmas. We had our longest stay in one place, three weeks, in San Diego. We went to a nearby church where people were interested to hear where we had come from. We had no trouble arriving in the RV. The 'parking lots' outside a lot of the churches there wouldn't look out of place in front of a shopping centre in England. The pastor and his wife took pity on us and offered to have the four children to play with their four children for the day. They went off seal-watching, along the beaches.

Geography and geology were big subjects for us as we travelled. To see what amazing things God has created and to be able to explain how things fit in around Noah and the flood was a good teaching time. We saw petrified wood (which looks like marble when polished), dinosaur footprints and fantastic rock formations. We made our way up the Pacific West Coast Highway visiting Death Valley, Yosemite National Park and the huge sand dunes of Oregon.

We saw elephant seals by the thousand on the beaches but had to wait until Seattle to see the whales which also travel up and down the coast. After a tour of the Boeing factory in Seattle we turned east and made our way across Montana, Wyoming and on to North Dakota. We visited the places we had read about in the *Little House on the Prairie* series by Laura Ingalls Wilder. At the end in July 2000 we returned to Florida and, leaving the RV to be shipped to Southampton, we flew back to the UK. The RV arrived safely, got through customs with no problems and we then lived in it while we sorted out what to do next and where to do it. As the children had grown up in the small market town of Newent on the Gloucester–Hereford border they always thought of us returning there to live. We had been very settled in the church there and the musical interest was still strong so it seemed a wise decision to continue to live there if Jonathan could find suitable work.

By the end of October it was getting cold and we found a house to rent in Newent with a driveway suitable for an RV and a big garden for the children. We unpacked all our furniture from storage and settled down to living in one place. Jonathon found work with Magnox Electricity doing a physicist/engineer job very similar to his previous position.

Matthew was now twelve years old and eager to get on with his piano and cello lessons. The Saturday music group was running a one year GCSE Music course so he joined in with a few other children. We gradually got in touch with a few other home educating families and the children soon picked up their friendships at church and music groups. One Christian home educating family was following the IGCSE course for natural science (with materials obtained from the Little Arthur School on the Isles of Scilly). Matthew also joined in and I took turns with the other mother doing the 'lessons' with five children. The local college of further education, Gloscat (Gloucestershire College of Arts and

Technology), was happy to have Matthew as a distance learning student for maths and English GCSE so he also started these courses, doing them in one year while he was aged thirteen to fourteen. They have since changed the rules and the door is now closed to under sixteen year olds. Daniel was still finding written work a real problem so GCSEs were definitely not the route for him. He signed up for an electronics course I saw advertised in the Education Otherwise magazine. It was an excellent hands-on project with a box of electronic goodies arriving each fortnight. The children have made good progress on piano, string and wind instruments. They have taken the musical grade examinations as I find having a goal to aim for does tend to focus their minds and increase the amount of practice. Matthew is now through the grades on piano, cello and oboe and the other three should all get to Grade 8 standard on their instruments over the next two years. Matthew, Daniel and Rosemary all play in the church music group and they continue to attend the Saturday music school and a midweek orchestra in which I also play.

Another useful resource for us has been a postal Bible school. They have all worked through various levels and the girls continue with this at the moment.

After his GCSEs Matthew was ready to go on to do A level music. The local comprehensive school in Newent accepted him as a part-time student so he wore sixth form uniform and joined in with the two other students who were taking A level music that year. He finished the course aged sixteen and then joined the sixth form officially to take English and philosophy A levels. He has been learning Spanish (at his request) for a few years and is taking Spanish A level at Gloscat, as the school does not teach Spanish. He has always wanted to study music and composition at a higher level and now has a place at Oxford University to read music.

Daniel has been at the local college for his 'sixth form'. He is studying music technology and photography and is also taking GCSE maths through the distance learning scheme. The college have been very supportive with his dyslexia – they formally assessed him and he has a special tutor who he sees once a week for help with planning his work.

Another major interest which has developed over the past few years for the girls and me is horse riding. We ride at a local farm where they have about twenty horses (some just foals) and over 600 sheep. In return for riding we help with the horses all year round and at lambing time we help with the sheep. Rosemary would like to work with horses and we plan to visit a local agricultural and equine college to see about a suitable course when she is sixteen. She has not taken GCSEs so far as she also has a problem with spelling and word recognition but it is not as severe as Daniel's difficulty. She has made good progress with her spelling and reading over the past two years and we are just thinking about the GCSE issue.

Heather is just like Matthew in that she reads voraciously and has no problem with spelling. She has followed his interest in music and Spanish and may want to go to university. At this time it would seem likely that she will do A levels but we have not at present decided about the necessity of GCSEs. As we have brought the children up in the Christian faith we have always tried to make sure that they know that they are special and loved just as they are. They don't have to pass tests to prove anything but sometimes exams are necessary to achieve a particular goal. We thank God for his faithfulness in keeping them close to himself and it has been a joy to see them all baptised over the past two years. Matthew has begun to find his feet in leading a young people's Bible study and speaking at a youth service. Daniel has discovered his niche playing violin in the church music group and taking his turn on the overhead projection system. The girls enjoy the youth singing group and Rosemary plays viola in the church band.

Matthew was eighteen in March and looking back we don't think we would have done anything differently. The time goes so fast and we only have the one chance to teach them and to encourage them to love and serve the God who we have found to be so real and so faithful.

Learning to Relax

- Peter and Fiona Phillips
- Children – one girl and one boy
- Aged nine and eleven
- Living in Dorset
- Have always home educated

So far, our home education experience has been a journey of discovery. It has not always been easy, but our journey has been very rewarding most of the time. We've asked a lot of difficult questions, we've read a lot of books and we've wondered where we were heading. God has led us on a path away from school systems and curriculum into a more relaxed family lifestyle, where education is a normal part of daily life. We're still travelling, but here is a reflection of where our home education journey began, and where it's taken us so far.

We are Pete and Fiona Phillips. We live in Poole, Dorset with our two children, Andrew who is eleven and Olivia who is nine. Olivia is known to all as Via, which is what Andrew called her when he was young, and it stuck.

Soon after Andrew was born, we began to consider playgroups, nurseries and schools. We discovered that, like many small schools, our tiny local school attached to the Parish Church had been shut down about ten years previously. The building was standing empty and forlorn. We found ourselves living between two large primary schools, both about three miles away. Further enquiries revealed that both schools ran an open-plan system, with up to ninety children sharing one area. We realised that our naïve expectation of a local community school with a Christian ethos and a gentle caring environment was, to say the least, unrealistic. Fiona's experience as a teacher before the children were born, only reinforced our conclusion that this was not what we wanted for our four-year-old.

We began to look at the possibility of a Christian school. At the time there was nothing in our area, so we visited one about thirty miles away. The atmosphere was lovely and the teachers welcoming, friendly and committed. However, we both found ourselves reflecting that it was still very much run on the same lines as any other school and somehow wasn't what we were looking for. What were we looking for? We really didn't know.

One day, visiting the local Christian bookshop, we were attracted by the cover of an issue of *Parentwise* magazine (May/June 1995). This was in mid-1996 – they were selling off old issues at a bargain price. We've never bought this magazine before or since, but for the sum of ten pence, we found ourselves reading a fascinating article that was to transform our lives. The article was by Stephen Richards, entitled 'Home Start: Is there any good reason why your child should attend nursery school?' At the end of the article he asks, 'So what happens when your child is five-years-old? The answer has to be, very little. There are no great educational reasons why five-year-olds should be in school. And a growing number of families have decided not to send their children to school at this age.'

This was a complete revelation to us both. We had never heard of home education before and we were both quite thrown by the idea. Were these children odd? Could they be a part of normal society? We contacted the Home Service, whose address was in the article, and discovered there was a home educating family in Bournemouth. We visited them. Aah . . . here was that elusive atmosphere we had been looking for: gentle, caring and Christian. We were also extremely impressed at their open and articulate children, in stark contrast to most other children we knew. The family moved away soon afterwards, but God had obviously touched our hearts because shortly before Via was born in September 1996 we remember telling people that our plans were to home educate and we gave up all ideas of nursery education as well. Our journey had begun.

Fiona continued to meet with other mums and their toddlers from church but, as Andrew reached his third birthday, his friends started their educational career at the local nursery schools. This marked us out as different, and brought us criticism, even from other Christians. It was probably the hardest moment of home education and this was two years before schooling was supposed to start at all! Amazingly, God intervened. Mark and Betty are a couple we had met at childbirth classes; we had vaguely stayed in touch via annual reunions. By this time they had a son and daughter the same ages as ours. We cannot remember how, but we got together and discussed our plans for home education. Betty was a trained nursery nurse and was concerned about the increasing pressure of early years education. Before we knew it, they too were planning to home educate and we were no longer on our own.

We knew no one except our two families who were home educating so we sent a short letter to *Home Time* magazine (edited by Sheila Barns). We were soon contacted by a loosely connected group of four families. Out of this grew the still-flourishing informal network of Christian home educators in Bournemouth, Poole and Christchurch. A key element has been 'home school mums', a coffee and discussion evening six to eight times a year. This was, and still is, a great source of mutual support and encouragement. From this small beginning we are now in touch with over twenty Christian home educating families in the area and there are usually new mums seeking advice from us 'old hands'. As relationships have grown between the families we all have a variety of opportunities for social contact but we have never established a regular group meeting for the children.

Now, six years after Andrew turned five-years-old, our understanding and vision have enlarged considerably. We started out thinking of home education in terms of 'reading, writing and arithmetic', but now we see it in terms of our overall lifestyle. All four of us are learning (not just the children), and we are learning all the time, wherever and whatever we are doing. Life cannot be divided into neat compartments of educational subjects – everything is interlinked, as we search out the purpose and destiny that God has for us. We worry less about gaps in the curriculum but pray for God to open the doors that will prepare each of us for the future. As the children get older we encourage them to share in the decision-making of how they spend their time.

For example, Andrew (who is now eleven) is choosing to devote considerable time to music, which has taken us by surprise because neither of us is at all musical. He started with the recorder and during the last year he has taken up violin and piano and has completed two music theory exams. He also enjoys listening to classical music and has learned a lot about the history of classical music from Aled Jones' CDs made in conjunction with Classic FM. We pray that God will help Andrew to use this interest in his service. Via (now nine) has a sensitivity to the needs of others and we encourage her in her desire to pray for them, both during services at church and at home. God is developing a caring heart in her.

We are sure that home education is part of God's plan for us as a family. The value of learning together is so much more than academic achievement. As we develop the lifestyle in which God is leading us, we can see the social and spiritual advantages, both for us and the children. Our focus is particularly on character development (often our own!) The lifestyle of home education gives us space and time to work through issues together and we can see that all four of us are developing maturity in Christ and in our relationships. We see this as a far more important outcome than academic success. We do not know what part exams might play over the next few years, but as both Andrew and Via are quite academically inclined we try to keep informed about the different paths they could take toward qualifications. Whatever route we might take though, we expect to judge our home education by maturity of character, rather than exam grades.

All relationships take time, and one of the most challenging parts of home education for us has been in making time to be together and develop our relationships. It is all too easy to focus on individual activities and miss opportunities to grow and share together. We are continually reminding ourselves to relax, to slow down and allow for time just to be in each other's company. After all, we are human beings, not 'human doings'! There is so much pressure, even among the home education community, to do as much as possible, for fear that others are doing more than you. One of the things we've noticed about our children is how much they enjoy simple play, especially when there is time because we have not over-booked or over-structured our week. Via spends considerable time in imaginative play with her Playmobil and other toys. They all have names and characters and there are days at a time when she builds up an ever-more involved scenario. This is an important and secure way for her to learn about the world around her and to explore people's reactions and relationships in different situations.

So, one of our main aims in home education is to capture each child's interest and excitement and allow them to learn through things that they can enthusiastically be involved in. We still make sure we cover the basics that we consider important, like maths and handwriting. Language skills happen very naturally because both children (and their parents!) are avid readers and love to talk and discuss at almost any opportunity. We had been leaving more advanced writing skills until they were older, but this year, Andrew was ready to tackle these. He already had a sound foundation of vocabulary, comprehension and study skills; all learnt naturally within the family setting. Now he is tackling the more mundane skills of spelling, grammar and punctuation. Reading aloud together, or on their own, we cover a wider range of topics, without specifically sitting down to study science, history, geography and so on. Our emphasis is very much on reading and discussion; we do not spend much time recording written work. Very often we find that in real life, all the subjects are interlinked, and our interest can easily carry us from one thing to another. As we've progressed on our home education journey, the most important lesson we've learned is to relax and to let God lead us gently on.

Over the years our vision has expanded. Home education has become a central theme, but our choices have changed our whole family lifestyle. Before Andrew was born, we knew Fiona wanted to stop working to focus on being Mum. Since then we have understood far more what an important calling it is to be a wife, a mother and a homemaker. More recently, Pete has reduced his working hours to four days a week, which gives us a much healthier balance to the week. Friday has become our family day. We go for walks and outings, when the world is not so busy.

We also have more time to prepare for making Sunday a special day. We are learning to make Sunday our day of rest and fellowship. To help the children become an active part of the church family, we worship together as they do not attend the junior church. In this way, not only are they actively involved on Sunday mornings, but their church role models are people who desire to move on with God. They see the reality of prophecy, prayer and preaching, and both of them have been able to bring readings and words of knowledge to the meeting. We look forward to leading them to discover their own personal calling from God, so that they will understand for themselves that he has a unique purpose and destiny for each one of us.

In no particular order, these are some of the books that have played an important part in our home education journey:

- Mary Hood, *The Relaxed Home School* (and other titles). As the title says, this is all about choosing to relax and allowing God to be in control. Mary Hood has encouraged us to experiment in education without curriculum.
- Robert Andrews, *The Family, God's Weapon for Victory*. This is not really about home education, but this is the book that inspired our vision for family life. Robert Andrews draws on the picture from Psalm 127, which describes our children as arrows in our quiver. Our job as parents is to trim those arrows as best we can, and then at the right time point them in the right direction and release them to fly straight and true into their own destiny.
- Raymond and Dorothy Moore, *Better Late than Early*. A classic home school title which gave us the confidence to avoid the peer pressure to find Andrew a place in the 'right' nursery school and so onto the first rung of the school system. The Moores provide ample evidence that early formal education is unnecessary.
- Nancy Lande, *A Patchwork of Days*. Real life experiences from a range of different home educators. Nancy Lande asked each contributor to describe one particular day in

their family's life, so the result is full of practical insights from everyday people.

- Susan Schaeffer Macaulay, *For the Children's Sake*. A gentle introduction to the nineteenth century educational ideas of Charlotte Mason. Most importantly, it recognises the God-given value of each child.

So, now the children are eleven and nine, we're about half way through our home education journey. I'm sure God has a lot more for us to learn – we haven't yet had to face the pros and cons of exams, further education and beyond – but we're confident that home education is an important part of God's calling for us. We don't have all the answers, but we've learnt that we don't need to be afraid to ask questions. When we started out we didn't know what we were looking for, but we kept on searching out our path and we're still doing so. Jeremiah 6:16 says 'stand at the crossroads and look; ask for the ancient paths, ask where the good way is and walk in it, and you will find rest for your souls.'

As we carry on our home education journey, we want to continue to seek out God's ancient paths. We aim, by God's grace, to train up our children in the way they should go, and to trust him that as they grow older they themselves will follow his path with perseverance.

Glossary

A level – Advanced Level, A levels are a subject-based qualification usually taken by students in the final two years of secondary education prior to possible university entrance. Students in England, Wales, and Northern Ireland can take any number of A levels in a wide range of subjects, but most students chose to study between two and four subjects.

BBC – British Broadcasting Corporation.

Covenant Christian School – independent Christian school in Stockport, England. A member of the Christian Schools Trust, the national support organisation for UK Christian schools.

Christian Education for Deeside (CED) – one of the oldest of the local support groups, CED has provided support and networking for Christian home educating families from a much wider area than Deeside. CED also runs the IGCSE/ O level examination centre in Rochdale.

Deut 6v7 list – a UK online mailing list for Christian home educators.

Duke of Edinburgh's Award – a voluntary, non-competitive and flexible programme of cultural and adventurous activities for all young people, whatever their background or ability.

Early Learning Centre – a UK retail chain specialising in toys and educational resources for younger children.

209

Education Otherwise (E.O.) is a UK-based membership organisation which provides support and information for families whose children are being educated outside school, and for those who wish to uphold the freedom of families to take proper responsibility for the education of their children.

GCSE – General Certificate of Secondary Education, GCSEs are a subject based qualification usually taken by school students at the age of sixteen but often taken by home educated children at other ages. Students in England, Wales, and Northern Ireland can take any number of GCSE examinations in a wide range of subjects. GCSEs were introduced in 1986 and largely replaced the previous O level examination.

Home Service – a Christian membership organisation concerned with promoting home-based learning and supporting those who currently home educate.

IGCSE – International General Certificate of Secondary Education, IGCSEs are subject-based qualifications usually taken by school students at the age of sixteen but often taken by home educated children at other ages. IGCSE examinations are offered by two examination boards – CIE (http://www.cie.org.uk) and Edexcel (http://www.edexcel-international.org). Though studied at a growing number of independent schools, IGCSEs cannot currently be offered by government-funded schools in the UK.

Key Stage – A Key Stage is a stage of the national education system in England, Wales and Northern Ireland, describing the educational knowledge, skills and understanding expected of students at the end of each Key Stage. The National Curriculum sets out targets to be achieved in various subjects at the end of each Key Stage.

LEA – Local Education Authority, the LEA is the department of a local council, or local authority, in England and Wales that is responsible for education within that council's jurisdiction.

National Curriculum – introduced into England, Wales and Northern Ireland, as a nationwide curriculum for primary and secondary government funded schools in 1988. The National Curriculum does not apply to independent schools or home-based learners.

NorthStarUK – online secondary learning community providing curricular and tutorial support for children aged 10–17+, (contact details can be found in the Curriculum providers and publishers list).

O level – Ordinary Level, O levels are subject-based qualifications which prior to the introduction of GCSEs in 1986 had been generally taken by school students at the age of sixteen. O level examinations are still available and are taken by some home educated children.

TEACH – The European Academy for Christian Home-Schooling, TEACH was set up to encourage and support the home education of children using the Accelerated Christian Education (ACE) curriculum, (contact details can be found in the Curriculum providers and publishers list).

Tearfund – is a leading relief and development charity, working in partnership with Christian agencies and churches worldwide to tackle the causes and effects of poverty.

Bibliography

Robert Andrews, *The Family, God's Weapon for Victory*, Wine Press Publishing, 1996, ISBN 1883893240.

Valerie Bendt, *How to Create Your Own Unit Study*, Family Learning Center/Common, 1990, ISBN 1880892421.

Rick Boyer, *The Hands-on Dad*, The Learning Parent, 1997, ISBN 0970877021.

James Burnett and Joe Ruston, *Getting into Medical School*, Trotman, 2006, ISBN 1844550745.

Children's Bible Hour, *Keys for Kids*, Children's Bible Hour, http://cbh.gospelcom.net/home.php, 2006.

Margaret Cousins, *The Story of Thomas Edison*, (Landmark Books), Random House, 1997, ISBN 0394848837.

Siegfried Engelmann, Phyllis Haddox and Elaine Brunner, *Teach Your Child to Read in 100 Easy Lessons*, Simon and Schuster, 1986, ISBN 0671631985.

Mary Hood, *The Relaxed Home School*, Ambleside Educational Press, 1994, ISBN 0963974009.

Nancy Lande, *Homeschooling: A Patchwork of Days: Share a Day With 30 Homeschooling Families*, Windycreek, 1996, ISBN 0965130304.

CS Lewis, *The Magician's Nephew*, Collins, 2000, ISBN 0006716830.

Susan Schaeffer Macauley, *For the Children's Sake*, Crossway, 1986, ISBN 0860654516.

Michael McHugh, *The Story of Inventions*, Christian Liberty Press, 1992, ISBN 1930092407.

L M Montgomery, *Anne of Green Gables*, Puffin, 1988, ISBN 0140324623.

Raymond Moore and Dorothy Moore, *Better Late Than Early: A New Approach to Your Child's Education*, Reader's Digest Association, 1989, ISBN 0883490498.

Loree Pettit and Dari Mullins, *Galloping the Globe*, Geography Matters/Christian Book Distributors, 1999, ISBN 193139721X.

John Pollock, *Shaftesbury: The Poor Man's Earl*, Hodder, 1985, ISBN 0340372818.

Mary Pride, *Mary Pride's Complete Guide to Getting Started in Homeschooling: A Practical Homeschooling Book*, Harvest House Publishers, 2004, ISBN 0736909184.

—, *Mary Pride's Big Book of Home Learning*, Master Books, 2005, ISBN 0890514593.

Arthur Ransome, *Swallows and Amazons*, Red Fox, 2001, ISBN 0099427338.

Brian D Ray, *Home Schooling on the Threshold – a survey of research at the dawn of the new millennium*, NHERI Publications, 1999, ISBN 0965755428.

Mark Roques, *Curriculum Unmasked*, Monarch Books, 1989, ISBN 1854240528.

Marian M Schoolland, *Leading Little Ones to God: A Child's Book of Bible Teachings*, Eerdmans, 1995, ISBN 0802851207 (Also available as a Banner of Truth edition, ISBN 0851510299).

John Hudson Tiner, *Isaac Newton*, Mott Media, 1981, ISBN 0915134950.

Laura Ingalls Wilder, *Little House on the Prairie*, Mammoth, 1992, ISBN 0749709308.

Dr J Wile, *Exploring God's Creation through General Science*, Apologia Educational Ministries, 2001, ISBN 1932012060.

Jessie Wise and Susan Wise Bauer, *The Well-Trained Mind: A Guide to Classical Education at Home*, W.W. Norton, 1999, ISBN 0393047520.

www.maths 2xl.co.uk, *Maths 2XL*, Maths 2XL Pty. Ltd, 2005.

Curriculum Providers and Publishers Referred to by Authors

A Beka Book, Inc

P.O. Box 19100, Pensacola, FL 32523-9100, USA
Email: international@abeka.com
www.abeka.org

Alpha & Omega

Alpha Omega Publications, 804 N. 2nd Avenue East, Rock Rapids, IA 51246, USA
www.aop.com

BBC Schools Radio production – Let's Move

www.bbc.co.uk/schoolradio/dance/letsmove

Bob Jones University Press

BJU Press, Customer Services, Greenville, SC 29614-0062, USA
Email: bjupinfo@bjupress.com
www.bjupress.com

Calvert School curriculum

10713 Gilroy Road Suite B, Hunt Valley, MD 21031, USA
Email: inquiry@calvertservices.org
www.calvertschool.org

Coordination Group Publications

CGP, Kirkby-in-Furness, Cumbria, LA17 7WZ, UK
Tel: 0870 7501262
Email: customerservices@cgpbooks.co.uk
www.cgpbooks.co.uk

Covenant Home Curriculum

N63 W23421 Main Street, Sussex, WI 53089, USA
Email: educate@covenanthome.com
www.covenanthome.com

Diana Waring

Diana Waring Presents! 621 SR 9 NE, PMB B-14, Lake
    Stevens, WA 98258, USA
Email: diana@dianawaring.com
www.dianawaring.com

Electronic Project

Sun House, 33 Church Lane, North Bradley, Trowbridge,
    BA14 6AZ, UK
Tel: 01225 760629
Email: new@kidstuff.co.uk
www.kidstuff.co.uk

Ginn

Customer Services, Ginn, Freepost (SCE 7554), PO Box 1127,
Oxford, OX2 8YY, UK
Email: enquiries@harcourt.co.uk
www.myprimary.co.uk

Greenleaf Press

3761 Hwy 109 North, Lebanon, TN 37087, USA
www.greenleafpress.com

Heinemann

Customer Services, Heinemann Educational, Freepost (SCE
6316), PO Box 970, Oxford, OX2 8BR, UK
Email: enquiries@harcourt.co.uk
www.myprimary.co.uk

Konos Inc

P.O. Box 250, Anna, TX 75409, USA
E-mail: info @konos.com
www.konos.com

Little Arthur Independent School

St Martin's, Isles of Scilly, Cornwall, TR25 0QL, UK
Tel: 01720422457
www.littlearthur.org.uk

NorthStarUK

Oaks Christian Centre, 4 Lea Road, Dronfield, S18 1SB, UK
Tel: 01246 410122
Email: info@northstaruk.org
www.northstaruk.org

Schofield and Sims Ltd

Dogley Hill, Fenay Bridge, Huddersfield, HD8 0NQ
Tel: 01484 607080
Email: post@schofieldandsims.co.uk
www.schofieldandsims.co.uk

Singapore Math

www.singaporemath.com
Distributed in Europe by Peter McGrath of Halfmoon Books
Email: halfmoonbooks@diginet.ie
www.halfmoonbooks.net

Sonlight Curriculum Ltd

8042 South Grant Way, Littleton, CO 80122-2705, USA
www.sonlight.com

T.E.A.C.H. (The European Academy for Christian Homeschooling)

Maranatha House, Unit 5, Northford Close, Shrivenham,
    Swindon, Wilts, SN6 8HL, UK
Tel: 01793 783783
Email: TEACH@christian-education.org
www.christian-education.org

Usborne Publishing Ltd

Usborne House, 83–85 Saffron Hill, London, EC1N 8RT, UK
Tel: 0207 4302800
Email: mail@usborne.co.uk
www.usborne.com